Falling Is Flying

Falling Is *Flying*
The Dharma of Facing Adversity

AJAHN BRAHM *and*
CHAN MASTER GUOJUN

EDITED BY
Kenneth Wapner

Wisdom Publications
199 Elm Street
Somerville, MA 02144 USA
wisdomexperience.org

Library of Congress Cataloging-in-Publication Data
Names: Ajahn Brahm, 1951– author. | Guojun, Chan Master, author. | Wapner,
    Kenneth, editor.
Title: Falling is flying : the Dharma of facing adversity / Ajahn Brahm and Chan
    Master Guojun edited by Kenneth Wapner.
Description: Somerville, MA, USA : Wisdom Publications, 2019. | Description based
    on print version record and CIP data provided by publisher; resource not viewed.
Identifiers: LCCN 2018020829 (print) | LCCN 2018036491 (ebook) | ISBN
    9781614294375 (e-book) | ISBN 9781614294252 (pbk. : alk. paper)
Subjects: LCSH: Suffering—Religious aspects—Buddhism. | Buddhism—Doctrines.
Classification: LCC BQ4235 (ebook) | LCC BQ4235 .A33 2019 (print) | DDC
    294.3/4432—dc23
LC record available at https://lccn.loc.gov/2018020829

ISBN 978-1-61429-425-2   ebook ISBN 978-1-61429-437-5

23 22 21
5 4 3 2

Cover design by Jess Morphew. Interior design by Gopa & Ted2, Inc. Set in
Athelas 10.85/14.8. Photo of Ajahn Brahm on page 135 is courtesy of the Ehipassiko
Foundation.

Wisdom Publications' books are printed on acid-free paper and meet the
guidelines for permanence and durability of the Production Guidelines for Book
Longevity of the Council on Library Resources.

Printed in the United States of America.

Please visit fscus.org.

In free fall, nothing is solid and there is nothing to hold on to. There is no way to control the experience. You have to surrender, and with that surrender comes the taste of liberation.

—MASTER GUOJUN

Instead of trying to discipline your mind with ill will, fault-finding, guilt, punishment, and fear, use something far more powerful: the beautiful kindness, gentleness, and forgiveness of making peace with life.

—AJAHN BRAHM

Contents

Editor's Note

IN 2016 Ajahn Brahm and Chan Master Guojun copresented in front of large audiences during Ajahn Brahm's Indonesian "Happiness Every Day" tour. *Falling Is Flying* is based on the teachings delivered at those joint appearances and on my subsequent conversations with Ajahn Brahm and Venerable Guojun.

The jumping-off point for the book was the painful controversies that both teachers faced. Ajahn Brahm's ordination of nuns led to his excommunication from the Thai Forest tradition of his teacher Ajahn Chah. He was essentially banished from Wat Nong Pah Pong, the monastery where he trained, and Ajahn Brahm's organization in Australia was stripped of its affiliation with Ajahn Chah's group.

Master Guojun was the target of a smear campaign. His case is complex, and, like Ajahn Brahm's excommunication, largely has to do with monastic codes, as well as the perception of what constitutes right action in the Buddhist world and the way money and power are exercised within religious communities.

Both these cases are litmus tests. How do Dharma masters respond when they are besmirched?

That was my primary question when I began building the book. But as I interviewed both monks and began constructing the chapters, the controversies they faced opened into a more free-ranging exploration of life's challenges and stories about their training—particularly their inimitable relationships with their teachers. I loved hearing their stories of the past, of the student-teacher / master-disciple bond. And my literary proclivities were awakened by their powerful evocations of the isolated and insular Buddhist worlds of their youth. Those unique environments are now being diluted by globalization and the internet, and I wanted to evoke them in their original strangeness and beauty for readers so they will not be completely lost.

The challenges Ajahn Brahm and Venerable Guojun faced in their training and then as accomplished Dharma teachers can help all of us find our way through the problems we inevitably face. We all want life to be other than it is. Yet, inevitably, we can't control what life throws at us. Both monks show us how to find strength and fortitude and keep an open heart regardless of circumstances. They are both inspirations *and* fully human examples of how to embrace the beauty of life with all its imperfections and difficulties.

Kenneth Wapner

PART I.
Caring Not Curing

Ajahn Brahm

1

Moving Toward Life—
No Matter How Difficult

IN 2009 a group of four highly qualified *bhikkhunis* asked me for full ordination. It wasn't unexpected; discussions about the discriminatory practices in our tradition had been ongoing. Full female ordination in Theravada Buddhism had been missing for about one thousand years, and I had been told that it was impossible to revive it on legal grounds. This may not have been a big issue in Asia, but it certainly was a problem in Western countries such as Australia, where I'm based.

The problem with ordaining bhikkhunis stemmed from their absence. The argument in Thai Theravada is that you need five fully ordained bhikkhunis to give full ordination to other bhikkhunis. If there were no bhikkhunis, as prescribed in the Vinaya (monastic code) to perform the ceremony, then ordination was impossible—a Catch-22. This was an embarrassment to many monks like me. It made me feel like a hypocrite every time that I mentioned that "compassion should be given to *all* beings." It was as if I was deliberately excluding women. As if my compassion was selective.

There were white-robed women, living in monasteries, following the additional eight precepts required of their gender, but they were assigned the same duties as white-robed men (*anagarika*) who were at the entry level to monastic life—duties often regarded by Western Buddhists as inappropriately menial. And whereas the men had the opportunity to proceed to higher ordination, the white-robed women were denied this option only because of their gender.

Attempts had also been made to establish a brown-robed order of ten-precept nuns, called *sayalay* in Myanmar and *siladhara* in the West. Because such an order of siladharas had no basis of legitimacy in the Theravada texts, they too became regarded as second-class monastics, not given the same respect and courtesies as the male monastics.

I was informed, for example, that the following five points were abruptly imposed by some senior monks on a community of siladharas residing within the same monastery, without the courtesy of consulting them first.

1. The most junior bhikkhu is senior to the most senior siladhara. This structural relationship is defined by the Vinaya and cannot change over time.
2. In public situations such as giving a blessing, leading the chanting, or giving a talk, leadership always rests with the most senior bhikkhu present. He may, if he chooses, invite a siladhara to lead, but this in no way establishes a new standard of shared leadership.
3. The bhikkhu sangha will be responsible for the

ordination and guidance of the siladharas, rather than the senior *ajahn*. Candidates should receive approval from the siladhara sangha, and acceptance from the bhikkhu sangha, as represented by the members of the elder's council.

4. The siladhara sangha should issue the invitation (*pavarana*) to the bhikkhu sangha at the end of the rains retreat, in accordance with the Vinaya.

5. The siladhara training is considered to be a vehicle respected in our tradition as suitable for the realization of liberation. It is complete as it stands and is not an evolution toward a different form, such as bhikkhuni ordination.

It is to be remembered that siladharas are outside the Vinaya and any rules found in the Theravada monastic code cannot be considered to apply to them.

These discriminatory and demeaning rules that relegated bhikkhunis to perpetual second-class status resulted in some female monastics abandoning monastic life altogether. Some moved to a different Western country, and some long-serving lay supporters departed in disgust.

When these four nuns formally asked me for ordination, my heart told me there was really only one response. It was unethical to refuse. That, as they say, is when the shit hit the fan.

Six months after my master Ajahn Chah sent me and my senior, Ajahn Jagaro, to Australia we established

Bodhinyana Monastery for monks. The next task was to create a monastery for nuns. In all the monasteries I had ever seen where monks and nuns mixed, the monks dominated. Women were forced into a subservient role. This was why I thought it was important to give the bhikkhunis a place of their own to practice, separate from Bodhinyana.

We searched for land and first found thirty-eight acres of scraggly ground, surrounded by farms, without the solitude and quiet required for contemplative practice. Bodhinyana was lovely, situated on over three hundred acres of wild forest and dramatic hills. It felt deeply disrespectful—and like more of the same—to shunt the women into this second-rate place. Then we learned of 538 acres of hills and beautiful forest with a river running through it in Gidgegannup, about eighty minutes from Bodhinyana. We managed to buy it, and Dhammasara was established.

Our bhikkhunis built it up. Ayya Vayama and nine other novices toughed it out those first years with rough accommodations and lean support. They had gained some independence, but still, they were not fully ordained, and they lived and practiced in a second-rate status to monks—in accordance with the Theravada tradition that dated back a thousand years, when the full ordination of bhikkhunis had, it was said, vanished from the earth.

After I became determined to ordain the bhikkhunis, I wanted to ensure that I was on sound footing according to the Vinaya. I taught myself Pali, which was structured a lot like the Latin that I had learned in school. As I delved into the canon, I became convinced of the conclusions of what's called "convergent theory," which assesses the text from various angles—linguistic, archeological, historical, political—and illuminates which parts of it were actually transcribed during the Buddha's lifetime and reflect the Buddha's own words and teachings and which parts were later additions. This was significant because it gave authenticity to the claim that teachings in the main books of the Dhamma-Vinaya tradition confirmed that ordaining bhikkhunis could be revived.

Careful research found that bhikkhunis had sailed from Sri Lanka to China in the fifth century CE to establish ordination there. That lineage was unbroken, according to the Vinaya. The Chinese are great record keepers. Clearly, the tradition of ordination the bhikkhunis had established there was authentic.

In Buddhism, we're monks first and belong to a particular sect of Buddhism second. It's the same for nuns. Monks and nuns would go from monastery to monastery and everywhere they went, in whichever monastery or temple they stayed, they were considered brothers and sisters.

The legitimacy of an ordination depends on fulfilling four factors:

1. The ceremony is performed within a monastic boundary and all members of the sangha permitted

to be in the gathering are present or have given their proxy beforehand.

2. The candidate for ordination is not prohibited from being ordained, for example because they are underage.

3. The formal act of ordination performed by the sangha, by a motion followed by three announcements, follows the standard formula in the Vinaya.

4. There are a minimum of five bhikkhunis, or ten bhikkhunis in the Middle Country of India (the Ganges Valley, approximately), at the ceremony.

It is to be noted that the fourth requirement does not mention that the quorum of bhikkhunis has to be from the same monastery or lineage or sect. As long as they are legitimate bhikkhunis, they fulfill the quorum.

The concept of different sects is called *nana-samvasa* in the Vinaya. There are only two legitimate grounds for a sangha to split into two sects in Buddhism: either people are excommunicated from a sangha by a formal act called *ukkhepaniyakamma* or they choose to leave. There are only two grounds for joining together again: either a sangha revokes an act of excommunication, or the people choose to come together. So, according to the Vinaya, five bhikkhunis from any tradition may choose to come together to perform the ceremony that creates a new bhikkhuni. The color of the robes and the rituals performed after the ceremony are all irrelevant to the legality of the ordination.

Thus, around eight hundred years ago, Theravada

bhikkhunis from Sri Lanka gave ordination to women in China, thereby starting the lineage of bhikkhunis in that land. The Sri Lankan bhikkhunis presumably returned to their homeland eventually, while their protégés in China evolved gradually, developing over the centuries the distinctive rituals and garments and interpretations that are now recognized as Mahayana. Importantly, they maintained the integrity of the ordination ceremony to fulfill the four factors unbroken to the present day.

A main point against ordination was the passage in the Pali canon where Ananda asks Buddha to ordain his stepmother, Mahapajapati Gotami. "If we ordain nuns, Buddhism will only last five hundred years instead of a thousand," Buddha is said to have replied, only acceding to Ananda's request after Ananda asks him if it is not true that women are just as capable of attaining enlightenment as men. This story does not appear in the Chinese and Sanskrit versions of the text, and I and others are quite sure that this is a later insertion into the canon and not something the Buddha, who famously never made predictions, said. And even if he did say it, he was obviously wrong!

Elsewhere in the scriptures, a strong argument was made for ordination. Soon after his enlightenment, Mara visited Buddha.

"Okay, I can see you're enlightened," said Mara. "But why teach? All it's going to do is give you headaches."

"I will not pass away until I have established the four pillars of Buddhism," Buddha replied. "The sangha of monks, the sangha of nuns, the community of experienced laymen, and the community of experienced laywomen."

Forty-five years later, Mara came to see the Buddha again, reminding him of his promise.

"You have succeeded," Mara observed. "There are thousands of monks and nuns and hundreds of thousands of lay followers. Now you can pass away." And three months later that is what Buddha did.

The Buddha's mission after enlightenment specifically mentions a sangha for women *equal* to the sangha of men. It was the whole purpose of his teaching.

My sangha and I were convinced that the full ordination of women did not break any laws. We brought five bhikkhunis from San Francisco to do the ordination, and they performed a beautiful, moving ceremony.

"At last! At last!" cried people in our sangha. "We liked Theravada Buddhism, but we hated the way you treated women."

People in our tradition had waited their whole lives for this. And now they were seeing it happen before their eyes.

For me, personally, now having fully ordained bhikkhunis was tremendously exciting. I felt Buddhism would be immeasurably enriched.

We have a tradition of great teachers who are women. One particularly dear to me is Patacara, also known as "Cloaked Walker." She ran off against her aristocratic parents' wishes with a good man from a lower class.

When she was pregnant with their second child, she asked her husband to take her back to her parents' village so they could assist with the birth.

The baby came early and she delivered midway through the journey. During the labor, a great storm struck. A snake bit Patacara's husband while he was cutting sticks for a makeshift shelter and he died. She delivered her baby and continued her journey. She came to a river crossing, swollen with rain. She didn't have the strength to ford it with both children in her arms. She carried her newborn across and was returning for her son when she saw a hawk circling overhead. She waved her arms, calling out, to shoo the hawk away. Her elder child thought she was signaling to him and moved toward her. He was swept away in the stream as the hawk plunged down and carried the newborn skyward.

Patacara continued toward her parents' village. They, too, had died in the storm after their house collapsed. News of her parents' death pushed her into madness. She tore at her clothes and her skirt fell off her. She became a cloaked walker—a madwoman in rags wandering through the countryside.

Patacara came upon the Buddha, teaching in the Jeta Grove. The congregation wanted to send her away, thinking, perhaps, that her partial nakedness would entice the monks. But Buddha commanded Patacara to recover her presence of mind. Her madness left her, and she worshipped at Buddha's feet. "Death of people we love is inevitable," said the Buddha. "It is a waste of life to brood or become bitter. No one can shelter us from the fate that awaits us. It is therefore incumbent that we set off on the path to nibbana."

Patacara took these words to heart and immediately asked to be ordained.

Her story does not end there. She became enlightened when the flame of her oil lamp was suddenly extinguished. Her poem in the *Therigatha*, the verses of enlightened nuns, ends with these lines:

> Lo! The nibbana of the little lamp!
> Emancipation dawns! My heart is free!

I was tremendously affected by this story. Here was a woman who had lost everything and yet was still able to discern wisdom and attain enlightenment. Her story seemed to me to be a perfect parable of the spiritual search: a giving up of life to attain life, a quest to find happiness and truth beyond the inevitability of suffering and the endless, heartbreaking cycle of birth and death. When the oil lamp blew out, that was the last little piece of Dhamma Patacara needed. My god, what she had been through!

Why can't we have these kinds of bhikkhunis around today, I wondered. Over the years that had been a recurring thought. And when I had my chance to make that happen I was determined not to let it go. I knew that I'd regret it for my whole life if I didn't respond to what my heart knew was right.

A week after the ordination ceremony at Bodhinyana, I was summoned to an assembly of monks at Wat Nong Pah Pong.

Wat Nong Pah Pong, or just Wat Pah Pong, is the main monastery in my teacher's lineage. It is in what could be considered the Bible Belt of Thailand—an extremely poor, flat, brutally hot backwater six hundred kilometers from Bangkok that borders Cambodia and Laos. Until recently, most of this region had no electricity or paved roads. That's changed, but not the region's religious fervor and conservative character, or the attitude among its clergy that they are the Republican Guard: the elite defenders of the faith and the hardest of the hard-core.

Three long flights brought me from Perth to Wat Pah Pong in the late afternoon. My summons coincided with the *kathina*, a ceremony for fundraising purposes at the end of the monsoon and the annual three-month rains retreat. Laypeople had been drawn from far and wide to make offerings, accumulate good karma, and listen to Dhamma talks that would go all night. My business preceded that marathon. I entered the large "discussion hall" at seven p.m. and took my place on the concrete floor, surrounded by a battalion of monks. The room's mood brimmed with hostility, even outrage.

It was already dark outside. The big room was stiflingly muggy and hot. All the windows were thrown open, but the air was dead. The lay community who had come for the kathina were not allowed into the hall—this was official monks' business in which they played no part. They gathered by the sills to eavesdrop—much more interested, I'm sure, in what was quickly clear would be my excoriation than the droning Dhamma to which they would be subjected through the night.

I was asked to justify my role in ordaining the bhikkhunis. When I had lived at Wat Pah Pong, my Thai had been fluent, but over the years it had deteriorated and become shabby. Imagine my difficulties in trying to explain the nuances in the Vinaya and presenting the case for the legality of my acts. But even if I had had the oratorial gifts of Cicero, I was doomed. The hostile elements had already made up their minds, and they drowned out the gentle voices that urged loving-kindness and compassion. I quickly realized that all argument was futile, but I nonetheless decided to dispute.

This took time. The inquisition lasted three hours. Finally, they made me an offer: formally state that the four women in Perth were not bhikkhunis and sign a statement to that effect, and then, they assured me, everything would return to normal. No punitive measures.

I took a moment to reflect in what was suddenly a very quiet room. People who were there said later that they thought I might have lost my breath. I was thinking! I recognized in myself a rather unseemly temptation to save my own skin. Yet I knew that I would never be able to live with myself if I recanted. And strong in my heart was the presence of the women I had ordained—how worthy they were, and how they had earned full ordination's rights and privileges.

The most junior of the four candidates had been keeping the ten precepts for over two years, whereas the senior had been maintaining her ten precepts for over twenty years. The senior had been a pioneer at Dhammasara Monastery in Perth, showing inspirational endurance by living alone for two years in a dilapidated caravan in the bush with no electricity, withstanding the extreme heat of the Australian summer and the cold winter mornings all without complaint. Had they been male, any monastery in the world would have felt privileged to have them in their community. Frankly, they were so impressive that they outshone most monks that I had met!

"I can't say these are not bhikkhunis. They are bhikkhunis," I said at last.

And that was that! They promptly excommunicated me and removed Bodhinyana and Dhammasara as affiliates of Wat Pah Pong.

A maelstrom erupted in the wake of the events at Wat Pah Pong. I was branded a renegade. I was suddenly out on my own, very exposed and reviled by a contingent of my fellow monks, some of them my Dhamma brothers. The whole episode influenced the way I teach and my appreciation of the Dhamma. And the ongoing controversy, which scandalized some in the Buddhist world, caused me to reflect on my acts.

Two moments had shaped the position in which I found myself. The first was the moment the bhikkhunis had asked for ordination. They stood before me not as emblems of the tradition in which I had trained and committed my life but as human beings. They asked for justice, a recognition of equality, what I felt were inalienable human rights. The second moment was when I had been asked to recant at the kathina assembly.

The impact of how such moments shape us was beautifully portrayed by novelist Joseph Conrad in *Lord Jim*. Jim is an idealistic first mate on a ship carrying Muslim pilgrims to Mecca. The ship hits something and begins to sink. The crew, including the captain, takes to the lifeboats, abandoning the sleeping pilgrims. Jim is torn between his moral duty to the pilgrims and fear for his life. In a moment of great confusion, not even conscious that he's doing so, Jim abandons ship, leaving the pilgrims to drown.

Except they don't drown. The ship doesn't sink and instead finds its way into port with the pilgrims still alive. Jim spends the rest of his days atoning for that one moment—that one act. He wanders the world, seeking redemption.

In both my Lord Jim moments, I could have jumped to save my skin. But my heart said otherwise. I knew that I couldn't have lived with myself. There were more important things at stake than my comfort and ease.

Years before the bhikkhuni ordination I had been meditating on Bunbury Beach one afternoon when a stone came whizzing past my ear. And then another.

"Hey, Rajneeshee! Get off our beach!" These words were obviously directed at me.

This was a time when Rajneesh, the notorious spiritual leader, had sent Sheela, his second-in-command, to Western Australia to establish a center.

I ignored the taunts. Another few stones flew past. It was only a matter of time before one struck me. So I rose and walked toward what I saw were a group of excited boys. This was the last thing they expected. They ran. All except one.

"I'm not a Rajneeshee," I explained. "I'm a Buddhist monk. Totally different religion."

One by one the boys returned, and we had a nice little talk about Buddhism.

In the punishing aftermath of the bhikkhuni ordination, I thought of those boys. Life sometimes throws stones at us. Friends push us away, belittle us, even try to hurt us. But we shouldn't run. We should move toward them with gentle determination. We need to listen to the prompting of our hearts and remain open, like Patacara, to a deeper understanding and a larger truth. That is what should *always* dictate our direction. We must always resolve to move toward life, no matter how difficult or even perilous that choice may seem.

2

Caring Not Curing

I HAD KNOWN JIVAKA (not his real name) since he was a little boy, when his family had emigrated from Sri Lanka to Perth. The father was a psychiatrist, and although Anglicized they were also devout Buddhists and came regularly to our temple in town. Jivaka went to the Dhamma School where I supervised the children, gave talks, and taught meditation.

Jivaka grew up in our temple and was a bright, hard-working, humble person. If he had any problems in his life, he would come and see me. He decided to follow his father into medicine, and when he was an intern, in his midtwenties, he asked to speak to me privately. I immediately saw that he was extremely distraught.

A young woman in his care had unexpectedly and suddenly died. He was shaken by her death, and the distress he felt was amplified when it fell to him to be the one to tell her husband that he no longer had a wife. He knew the husband would have to tell two young children that they had lost their mother. He felt that he had failed this young family: they had placed their trust in him, and he had failed them.

"I want to resign," he told me, "give up medicine. I don't think I could go through something like this again. I have realized that I'm not cut out to be a doctor. Still, before I handed in my resignation, I wanted to come talk to you."

I felt his pain and confusion. How hard the experience had been for him! But I wasn't ready to let him off the hook. The fact that he cared, and cared so deeply, I knew, would make him a good doctor—a better doctor, in fact, than someone more detached and unfeeling. I looked at him for a long moment. He was drowning in sorrow and shame.

"You have misunderstood the purpose of being a doctor," I finally replied. "If you think the purpose of practicing medicine is to cure people, you will fail over and over and over and go through the same anguish you're experiencing now. The purpose of being a doctor is not to cure your patients. It is to *care* for them."

It was as though the burden that had been weighing on his heart lifted. He understood what I was getting at straight- away and went back to work and eventually became a gastroenterologist. A few weeks ago one of my monks had to have an endoscopy, and guess who did it? My old student Jivaka. Out of gratitude, he waived his fees.

You can *always* care for people even if you can't cure them. Some of Jivaka's patients will undoubtedly die. But if he knows that he has cared for them, that changes everything. They will be more likely to die peacefully, comforted by the care they have received. The pain experienced by the people who love them won't be as severe. They will know that the person they loved was cared for at the end. And, although I have no statistical proof, I think that it's pretty obvious: when you make care your first priority, you're also more likely to cure.

Compassion is a form of caring. Kindness and compassion. Compassion and kindness. We could sum up the core teachings of Buddhism and just about any other religion in those two words. Compassion can be more potent than the most powerful drugs. When we truly care, when we are in the moment with a compassionate heart that is fully engaged and fully present, we can help alleviate at least some small part of the suffering in this world.

Jivaka's wife volunteers for an organization called ASeTTS (Association for Services to Torture and Trauma Survivors). Its purpose is to deal with those refugees who have managed to find physical freedom in a country like Australia, but whose minds are still in cells where they are being tortured, abused, and raped. They are not really free at all.

I was invited to give a talk at ASeTTS. I asked why in the world they had invited me. I was surprised when I was told that many of the psychiatrists and psychologists who worked there had come to my Friday night talks. They had adopted many of my teachings to help traumatized refugees.

I asked what story helped the most. And they told me they had used something from my book, *Opening the Door of Your Heart*. They had adapted it to fit what so often appeared to be the irreparably damaged hearts and souls of the refugees ASeTTS serves.

At some point in treating trauma, when the trauma victim they were treating felt safe, they led her through the following visualization exercise:

Imagine your heart in your chest. Imagine it as a Valentine's Day heart, a nice pink or red heart as it would appear on any greeting card, not your real heart. Imagine there is a little door in your heart, and that the door can swing open. Inside your heart, imagine a part of yourself that you feel comfortable with. A part of you that is a happy, free, healthy person, that is smiling, relaxed, and full of life. Then look down toward the floor at your feet. There are many people there who are being tortured. They are crying out in fear and pain. See those suffering people as parts of yourself that are now outside you, small and helpless and despairing at your feet.

Imagine a stairway being lowered from the door in your heart where the whole and trusting and happy person is standing. The stairway stretches down to the ground. The whole, happy person standing in the door of your heart holds out her hand for the damaged, despairing, terrified people on the ground below who have been tortured and raped. "Come into the door of my heart," she says. And those terrified people, shaking with fear, walk up the stairs one by one. The door is wide open, and she embraces each person and says, "Come in. Do not be frightened. You are part of me. You can come home."

When those terrified, suffering parts of yourself are invited to come into the door of your heart, when they are shown care and compassion, a huge change is possible. You can be at peace with your past, at peace with life. You can never forget what you've endured, but you don't need to be traumatized by it ever again.

To move beyond life's traumas and disappointments we need to open the door of our hearts to all of life—to the sickness and pain and fear and horrendous experiences some of us have had to endure.

It's counterintuitive. Our instinctive reaction is to run away from pain. But the only way to attain freedom is not to run away but to bring the pain in, to embrace it, and to accept it into the most tender, open, vulnerable, feeling part of ourselves.

When I gave my talk at ASeTTS I overheard a woman who had been repeatedly raped describing her experience to a young man. The young man was understandably shocked.

"What you're describing makes my skin crawl. It's horrible! Disgusting."

She came back fast and hard. "NO! You can't say that about me. It's made me who I am. You can't say it's terrible. And I won't say it's terrible."

She was no longer ashamed or traumatized. There was no stigma. She was free! She had made peace with life.

When you meet a person like that, they're powerful. They shine. They are magnificent. They really deserve to be called *awesome*.

3

The Wind of Wanting

THE CAUSE OF HAPPINESS is stillness.

My teacher Ajahn Chah would wave his hand like a wildly blowing leaf. He said when the wind dies the leaf comes to a default state of stillness. The leaf is like our minds, which only move with the wind of wanting, even if that wanting is for something good! Let go of all wanting and the mind stills. It is a mountain lake that reflects the moon and the stars.

Pick up a glass of water. Try to hold it perfectly still so the water doesn't move. You can't! It doesn't matter how hard you concentrate or how long you try. Yet through the boundless wisdom and compassion of the Lord Buddha, there is a way: *put the glass down*. The great wonder of the Dhamma is revealed. The water becomes perfectly still all by itself. It only moves because you grasp it.

At Wat Pah Pong I lived in a small hut on stilts, perhaps two by three meters. It was floored with uneven planks that the villagers had sawed by hand. The floor was full of gaps that let the mosquitoes in. I slept on a thin straw mat.

At three o'clock each morning the bell rang, summoning us to the Dhamma hall to chant and meditate. I walked barefoot through the warm, fine sand from my little hut in the dark. The jungle was an impenetrable wall of deeper darkness on either side of the narrow path. A few cicadas hummed in the blackness, giving the familiar background music to the last hours of the night. All else was quiet. A couple of big candles on the wide altar were enough to let the assembling monks shuffle safely to their mats. Two larger-than-life brass Buddha statues glowed in the candlelight. There was no reason for having two statues other than that two were donated. Their number and size was often a disappointment to me, as they had to be polished every fortnight by the junior monks. I was one of those junior monks and the polishing took several hours. One statue would have sufficed, I often thought—a small one, preferably not made of brass. The chanting was an endurance test too, but the meditation that followed was peaceful. That was because I usually fell asleep. I was sleep deprived, malnourished, and trying to be aware in a humid and hot climate that I was not designed for. I was "Made in London." There were no fans or air conditioners or dehumidifiers. There wasn't even any electricity. Just the warm, numbing, consciousness-strangling, heavy blanket of the motionless jungle air.

Dawn came and we set off for the village and our alms rounds. We collected our one meal for the day. The quality was such that we usually didn't want another. Rice, frogs, ant soup, snails, water buffalo afterbirth. It kept you alive—just.

That part of Thailand had never been colonized. It was a pure, indigenous culture. Life went on as it had for centuries. The seasons rolled around. We called them "hot," "very hot," and "hot and wet." Dirt roads ran off into nowhere. There was no electricity. The raised houses of the villagers were like slightly larger versions of my hut. The water buffalos that were used to work the paddies huffed softly through the night beneath the raised floors where families ate, talked, and slept.

Sometimes I would walk back to Wat Pah Pong at night through the village after doing a funeral service. In house after house, I would see the same scene: fifteen or twenty people seated on the floor around an oil lamp. The light was just enough to see a semicircle of golden faces. All generations, from young children to grandparents, sitting around telling stories. This was what the whole family did each night. There was nothing else. Just being together.

In some of these remote villages, I was the first white man they had ever seen. It was a beautiful, old culture—very beautiful, but all gone now.

In my first or second year as a monk, I became ill with scrub typhus, which was spread by a little mite living in the forest floor. According to the health department in Bangkok, there was no scrub typhus in our part of Thailand. That was because all the locals had developed immunity against it. But when we Westerners came there, we got it straightaway.

My fever was very high, perhaps 104 degrees, with terrible aches and pains. I was sent to the hospital. This was 1975 in a remote backwater of what was then still very much a third-world country. It was the most rudimentary of hospitals, and I was in the most ill-equipped and understaffed part of it—the monk's ward.

Six beds were lined up on either side of the room. A nurse was stationed next to the door. At six in the evening the nurse vanished and at seven no one had taken his place. I asked the monk in the next bed if we should we tell someone the night nurse hadn't arrived.

"There is no night nurse," he replied. "If something happens to you in the middle of the night, they figure it's just your bad karma."

There was a bed pan next to the bed that was soon filled up. No one emptied it. We had to do that ourselves. I was so weak that I could barely stand up, let alone carry a full bed pan to the toilet. And my fellow monks were in a similar or even worse condition, stricken with cholera, malaria, and hepatitis. There was no way we had the wherewithal to help each other.

I lost track of time. Twice a day I received a shot—a cocktail of antibiotics administered in my bum. This was a long time before the invention of single-use needles. These needles had been recycled again and again and again. First they had been used in Bangkok, where the wealthy people lived. Then they were shipped to the boonies where we were and used on ordinary people.

Only then were they deemed fit for monks. We were supposed to be tough guys.

The needle they used on me was really, really dull. And the nurse who gave me those shots twice a day was not a pretty, petite nurse in a nice, clean uniform. This nurse was in late middle age and built like a water buffalo. She had to be that strong because the needle she used was so incredibly dull. She brought it up past her ear and stabbed straight down with force, *whack*, right into my bum. And even though I was supposed to be compassionate . . . well, not to that woman. My ass got really, really sore.

I guess the antibiotics kept me alive, barely, but I was not by any means improving. It was as if my life force were slowly leaching away.

That's when Ajahn Chah came to see me. At the very sight of him all my aches and pains instantly vanished. My master! He had come to visit me in my moment of need. He had taken the time. He cared. I looked at him with love and devotion, preparing in my mind what I thought was a suitably stoic monk-like but realistic assessment of my condition for what I was sure would be his solicitous concern. Instead, the Dhamma he gave me was like a swift kick in the nuts.

"You'll either die or recover," he said. And then he was gone.

That was *not* what I wanted to hear.

As his robes disappeared through the door, the nurse appeared. *Whack!*

By this time, I could not lie on my back—it was too

painful. My ass felt like someone had been using it as a pin cushion. I couldn't see down there but I could feel ever so gingerly the welts and scabs from those filthy needles. I curled on my side in a whimpering miasma of misery and despair. *You'll either die or recover.* I turned over Ajahn Chah's prognosis in my head. Was that all he had for me? How heartless he had been! As I replayed his words, it slowly dawned on me that I had been *wanting* to get well. I had been fighting the sickness. When I realized that, I decided to stop fighting and let go. To put down the cup.

In a few minutes I couldn't feel my body anymore. Not even my bum. I was having a wonderful time.

That's when the fever stopped. To let the mind rest and be still—to stop the wind of wanting—gave my body a huge therapeutic boost. Finally, I felt at peace, and the shaking stopped. My mind was still and my body relaxed. I was happy.

4

Putting Kindness First

BODHINYANA MONASTERY came into being about half a year after Ajahn Chah had a stroke that left him mostly paralyzed. When Ajahn Chah had sent me to Australia to assist Ajahn Jagaro in founding a monastery for students in Perth, I had assumed it was for a year or two and that I would be recalled to Thailand or sent somewhere else. Ajahn Jagaro would stay behind to lead the group. It didn't work out that way. Ajahn Chah was unable to talk or move. He couldn't recall me! Which is why I've been stuck Down Under among the kangaroos and koalas for all these years.

When we first arrived in Australia, Ajahn Jagaro and I stayed in the hectic city environment of Perth. We missed the peace and quiet of the forests of Northeast Thailand, the space and contemplative solitude of the life we had loved at Wat Pah Pong, Ajahn Chah's monastery. We wanted to establish our own monastery in the Thai Forest tradition—and for that we needed a forest! Once or twice a week, we would drive into the countryside with members of our sangha, looking for pieces of land on which to build a monastery and retreat center that would be removed from the hustle and bustle of the city and would be a good place for meditation.

We looked and looked; nothing seemed quite right. We didn't want to be too far from Perth, which would have made it difficult for our followers to come to see us. It would have been a problem for us as well. For instance, our monastic code prohibits us from cooking. I'm not sure how the Australians in what was then a very rural part of the country would have responded to Thai Forest monks in orange robes with shaved heads coming out of the bush and silently standing before them, begging bowls outstretched. And I wasn't keen to find out. We didn't want to starve, so we needed to be close to our sources of support while still far enough away to have the tranquil natural environment that has been part of our tradition and practice for millennia.

We finally found what we were looking for in the forested hills in Serpentine (named for the river that runs through it—not snakes). The hills rose several hundred feet off the coastal plain and continued inland for a number of miles before dropping down into the outback—the vast, mostly empty interior of the continent.

The spread we looked at was fairly large. The owner had been trying to run sheep and cows on it, but it was so hilly and full of rocky outcrops that he couldn't find his sheep when he wanted them. That was perfect for us—not being found is precisely what we Forest monks like.

As usual, we were dirt poor. Was it even worth making an offer? The owner was asking $200,000 for about 130 acres. We had $90,000. We finally decided to bid it on the off chance . . . Lo and behold, the owner accepted! He must have been really fed up with his wayward sheep.

The purchase left us with no money and a rough, unimproved parcel. Ajahn Jagaro and I scavenged two old doors from the local landfill and put them on bricks. That's what we slept on. Because Ajahn Jagaro was my senior, he got the smoother, less battered door. But my door had a secret advantage; it had a hole in the middle. I highly recommend this brilliant design feature. I didn't need to get out of bed to go to the toilet at night!

We slept on our doors, camped in the forest, very much in the manner to which we were accustomed in Thailand.

In that first year, we had very little support. We found out later that the Buddhists in Perth were waiting to see if we were real monks and would stay the course. Once they saw we were in it for the long haul, they knew it was in their interest—and their children's interest—to support us.

During this period Ajahn Chah's condition remained stable. Even before the stroke immobilized him, it was clear he wasn't well. He had dizzy spells and doctors diagnosed fluid on the brain. Even with his neurological problems, he didn't seem old. He was always strong and bright. I had received such great teaching from him over the years. I was grateful, and he had taught us not to be attached. His imminent departure was no big deal.

We thought he would soon be gone. The monks in

Thailand met and decided not to have any medical intervention. Just let him go. The king of Thailand had other ideas. He insisted we keep Ajahn Chah alive and paid for round-the-clock care and all the other support that was needed. Which is why Ajahn Chah lasted another nine years. He was unable to walk or speak, and he was mostly paralyzed.

There was always a medic on duty and two attending monks. At one point the medic was afraid Ajahn Chah had died. He had stopped breathing. The medic knew Ajahn Chah was going to die one day. He just didn't want it to be on his shift. He wanted to try to resuscitate him, but the monks on duty said to leave him alone. They could see he was in deep meditation.

The medic had a hard time believing that. Ajahn Chah looked dead. So the medic argued with the monks. They agreed on a compromise. He would take blood samples every three minutes or so to ensure that enough oxygen was going to Ajahn Chah's brain and other organs. He took the blood samples, and indeed for one hour and then two hours Ajahn Chah's blood continued to be well oxygenated, although he did not appear to be breathing. The only way to do that is to get into what we call the fourth *jhana*, a very deep meditative state. Ajahn Chah couldn't walk or speak. But he could still meditate.

It took three or four years to begin to think about erecting the meditation hall at Bodhinyana. By that time, I had some building experience from putting up simple structures around the property. My sangha had confidence in me because they saw what we had done already. They were also impressed that we were building simple rather than elaborate structures, and it would obviously save a huge amount of money for me to do the work on the building.

When it came to the hall's design, I was still the number-two monk. Ajahn Jagaro was Bodhinyana's abbot. I was his assistant. We spent ten days arguing over the building's siting and proportions. The arguments grew increasingly heated. I was ashamed: we were acting like laypeople! Like husband and wife! It came to the point where we stopped talking to one another. We just left peevish notes. One point of contention was the direction the hall would face. Looking back, it seems crazy. But when you're in the midst of an argument, your position can seem really, really important. I'm embarrassed to say that there was actually very little difference between his plan and mine.

I finally came to my senses. I told myself that as a monk my duty was to teach people to live in peace and harmony and practice compassion and nonattachment. Why was I seemingly incapable of acting that way myself?

I went to Ajahn Jagaro's room. When you say you're sorry in Thailand, it is a tradition to offer candles, incense, and flowers to the person you're seeking forgiveness from.

I presented my tray of gifts to Ajahn Jagaro. "I've come here to apologize for my speech and actions these last days," I said. "I am truly sorry. We should never argue."

I could see all the tension drain from him. He was amazed and touched.

"But I'm going to ask for a bit of a favor," I added.

The softness that had come into his face changed. He looked apprehensive and wary, as though I had tricked him!

"I agree to follow your plan. But please let me be the builder. I still think your way is the wrong way. But I want to do it your way because I think it will be a wonderful practice for me."

He was clearly moved. He had been expecting me to say, "Go ahead and do it your way. But I don't want to be involved."

I spent the next year building our meditation hall at Bodhinyana, setting yellowish-pink brick in beige mortar. We chose the brick because it was not too expensive but still looked good. It had an earthiness about it. I laid a lot of brick.

Brick by brick—I wasn't just talking about letting go. I was actually doing it! I was building something I thought was second rate. It didn't matter. Brick by brick I learned that you don't have to do it the way you think is best. You have to do it the way that is the *kindest*. I built that lesson inside me in the same way that I built the meditation hall.

Perhaps six months before his stroke, before he sent me to Perth, Ajahn Chah said: "I have built many monasteries. But I haven't built many monks. What is most important is to build people. Not temples." When he said this, his voice and his face were full of pathos.

I still think my way would have been the right way to build the meditation hall. But in everything we do we should always put people first, not our ideas about the right way or the wrong way. Candles, incense, and flowers. Kindness is always available to us.

5

There Is Nothing

WHEN I FIRST decided to become a monk in 1973, I was a schoolteacher, and I didn't want to leave my students and colleagues in the lurch. So I resolved to wait for the end of the school year to leave for Thailand, where the plan was to shave my head and become ordained as quickly as possible. But, as they say, you can't keep a good monk down (even an aspiring one). In the dreary English dawns before the school day began, I sped happily on my motorbike to a Thai temple in London to participate in the morning chanting. More often than not, I would wake the resident monks. I could hear them muttering under their breath as they rose groggily to my summons: *Not this guy again. What is his problem?*

Most of the people I knew were incredulous. *A monk? In Thailand? No way! You'll never be able to stick it out. Wait and see. You'll be back.* Unfortunately, most of those people are dead now, and I can't say I told you so.

I was ordained as a novice in Bangkok. The first few nights after ordination I had a recurring nightmare: I dreamed that I was no longer a monk. The relief and joy I felt were indescribable when I woke to see my robes and realize that, yes, I was still a monk after all—it had only been a dream.

How can I have been so completely sure about this path? What impelled me, a trained scientist from a secular background? My family had absolutely no association with Buddhism.

Most of us in the West have a hard time accepting the reality of reincarnation and the causality of karma. But I am certain that my overwhelming attraction to Buddhism came from my association with Buddhism in my past lives. Karma compelled me to shave my head and cherish those robes.

Six to eight weeks after being ordained as a novice in Bangkok, I saw an absolutely filthy-looking group of monks who were in the city taking care of their visas. These were jungle monks, I soon learned. Being from a proper English household where we were scrubbed behind the ears and wore starched clothes, I was naturally enchanted. Among this group of jungle monks was Ajahn Sumedho, an American monk about twenty years my senior. I introduced myself to him and asked how he had come to be so deliciously grubby. He invited me to come with them to Wat Pah Pong to meet his teacher, Ajahn Chah.

We traveled six hundred kilometers by overnight train from Bangkok into the backwater of the Northeast, finally arriving at the monastery's gates. My first impression of Ajahn Chah was negative; I was utterly unimpressed. He was making a papier-mâché mountain as part of the commemoration ceremony for his mother's recent death. I still don't understand the rationale behind this odd creation. A papier-mâché mountain? Why? But that wasn't what put me off. As part of the commemoration, we were set to work weaving grass baskets. Ajahn Chah came over and complimented me on my efforts. I looked around. My basket left much to be desired, especially compared to the competition. I had the strong sense that Ajahn Chah was trying to be ingratiating and endear himself to me through flattery. *This guy's a phony!* Or so I thought.

What changed my mind was interesting. Through an interpreter, another novice monk, Gary from Los Angeles, was asking Ajahn Chah questions. I was in earshot and I eavesdropped on the conversation. Something strange began to happen. Ajahn Chah kept giving answers that had nothing to do with the questions that Gary had asked. But his answers perfectly corresponded to the questions that I was internally, silently asking Ajahn Chah in my mind!

At first I thought this seemingly telepathic call and response was completely coincidental, yet as it continued it became increasingly difficult for my scientifically trained mind to dismiss it as chance. I kept thinking of questions and Ajahn Chah kept answering them. It was uncanny—spooky and wonderful at once—and it went on for a full ten minutes. Gary, who thought Ajahn Chah was being completely unresponsive, was obviously nonplussed.

It was an intriguing, convincing performance. I asked if I could stay at Wat Pah Pong, and Ajahn Chah said yes.

So began my long period of training with my teacher. I moved into my little hut with my robes, alms bowl, and mosquito net, and joined the monastery's timeless routine. I walked the paths of warm, powdery sand through the monastery's jungly quadrants. I rose hours before dawn each morning to chant and meditate in the big, candlelit hall. I tried my best to meditate all night once a week, although I rarely managed that and nodded off, my head slumping into my chest.

The emphasis in this austere and simple life was on meditation. That was exactly what I wanted. The bliss I had experienced with my early meditation experiences had hooked me. It was so much stronger than even the great sex that my girlfriend and I had in Gloucester before I took my monastic vows! Meditation was so much more pleasurable and longer lasting. One taste of it, and I was addicted. I became a meditation junkie, and I still am.

Meditation is more powerful than the greatest art. Beethoven may move and transform us. Our minds may soar. But never as much as in meditation. If you're a Catholic and you have union with God, they make you a saint. If you're a monk, they say, "Perfectly normal. Carry on."

We were only supposed to sleep four hours in any twenty-four-hour period. I never was quite able to do that (I got it down to four and half hours at one point). It was a grueling, exhausting regimen. But it didn't feel that way. My underlying mood was buoyant. I was incredibly happy. There in the obscure backwater jungles of Thailand, about as far from England both physically and psychically as it was possible to get, my life was magical: a steady stream of insight, peace, and bliss.

Early on in my sojourn at Wat Pah Pong, Ajahn Chah sent me on a mission that really helped me with my meditation practice. Bung Wai village wanted to found a monastery, and Ajahn Chah sent six of us Western monks to assist them. There was no building in Bung Wai for us to stay in, and Ajahn Chah directed us to encamp on the village's cremation grounds.

When we slept we were allowed to use our mosquito nets, which we rigged with our umbrellas. Snakes slithered by. After a while as a Thai Forest monk you get so that you have no fear of snakes. I quite honestly felt love and empathy for them! Even the ever-present, deadly cobras. We monks joked that there were one hundred species of snakes in Thailand: ninety-nine of them are venomous, and the other strangles you.

I once saw a king cobra cross a jungle path. With my scientist's eye, I measured the snake as it slithered along the path in front of me. I counted each of its lengths and calculated it was roughly fifteen meters. Was it supernatural? I can't say for sure.

Ajahn Chah would come every evening to the cremation ground to do a two-hour meditation and give a talk. It showed his support and interest in the place.

We began the meditation at six o'clock. This was exactly the time when the mosquitoes became active. We had to remain perfectly still during meditation, and we have a precept against killing, so there was no swatting them away. We had no coils, and we were not allowed to use our nets.

Those mosquitoes ate us alive. There is no other way to say it. Can you imagine? I would count sixty or seventy on my body at once, their little bodies slowly puffing up with my blood.

We Westerners watched awestruck as the Thai monks were able to sit perfectly still and remain comfortable during this excruciatingly itchy feeding frenzy. How did they do it?

I learned how—by necessity. After my body was paved with bites, I began to be able to focus deep inside myself, so I couldn't feel my body anymore. During those two-hour sits, the mosquitoes taught me how to keep my mind from wandering. Once I was deep inside, it was as though they were not there. And, in fact, this is not just an illusion. In deep meditation, your respiration slows. There is barely any carbon dioxide coming out of your pores. And it is the carbon dioxide exuded by your body that attracts mosquitoes!

Sitting in the cremation grounds of Bung Wai, we Western monks learned how to become invisible. I think Ajahn Chah, although he never indicated it in any way, mightily enjoyed that process.

You never had a clue what Ajahn Chah was up to. The way he reacted was often completely unexpected. I've met a couple of Nobel laureates in my day, and compared to Ajahn Chah they were dullards. An abbot only has the power his disciples give him. Ajahn Chah's disciples included the king and queen of Thailand and the poorest of illiterate villagers. He could relate to them all.

One instance of his unpredictability that has stayed with me involved an exorcism. A woman was brought to him in a deranged state, swearing, frothing from the mouth, making wild, contorted movements. Ajahn Chah took a look at her. "She's possessed by a very dangerous spirit. Dig a hole. Boil water. We need to pour boiling water over her and bury her!"

The woman instantly came out of it. A minute later, she was sitting quietly in front of Ajahn Chah, no longer possessed but spitting mad, infuriated because she thought he was really going to boil her alive!

I never knew what he would do next, and he often acted as though I weren't there. I had very little one-on-one teaching from Ajahn Chah.

An exception to this was, perhaps, seven or eight years after I had become a monk. One of Ajahn Chah's Western affiliate monasteries had bought a sauna for Ajahn Chah in the hope of luring him there to give a talk. Two-thirds of Ajahn Chah's talks were absolute rubbish, but every once in a while he'd spit forth a real rip-snorter.

As he was coming out of the sauna, I was walking in the opposite direction. We were going to pass. I was proud that my mind was so peaceful and pure, and I silently invited him to take a look inside my head with what I knew were his remarkable powers of telepathy and admire the pristine nature of my gray matter.

I had a keen intuition that this was going to be a special meeting. It was destined that we should so meet—a meeting of remarkable men. Ajahn Chah had singled me out. He held me to be important and special. A monk among monks. He knew that I had worked hard and done all the right things. Now it was time for transmission. I was sure that this was going to be momentous.

He stopped and looked at me. "Brahmavamso," he said. "Why?"

I was dumbfounded. "I don't know," I stammered.

He laughed. When you're absolutely stupid, they don't scold you. They think it's funny! He was deeply amused.

"If anyone asks you that question again, the answer is: 'There is nothing.' That is the answer to that question. Do you understand?"

"Yes, yes! I understand."

He smiled at me and shook his head in the way you would to a three-year-old. "No, you don't," he said.

I felt so incredibly stupid. I shall always remember it: exactly the place, precisely what was going through my head. It was the most personal instruction he gave me. *There is nothing*. Nothing to understand? No answer to the question *why*? Why what, for goodness' sake?

I turned his words over and over. If he could read my mind, which is what I had deliberately been inviting, was he responding to what was in there? The encounter haunted me. It took me many, many years to discover its meaning. So I leave it to you to ponder . . . as I did.

6

Free-Range Frog:
Living Simply and Gratefully

THE COLLECTION of alms is one of the fundamentals of the Theravada Thai Forest tradition of Buddhism and goes back to the Buddha's time.

The point of the alms bowl is that we eat what we're given. We don't get to choose. We give up control and give thanks in response. Our gratitude is very real. We are not allowed to cook or prepare our own food. Without alms we would literally starve. We owe our lives to the alms givers. By subsisting off alms, we choose to live a way that is both humbling and liberating. But it can also be disgusting! How many meals did I have in Northeast Thailand of frog soup? The villagers were so poor that this was literally all they had to give us.

The recipe for frog soup is simple. Gather small frogs from the puddles in the rainy season. Each frog should be just big enough to fit in a Chinese spoon. Boil the frogs in water. No salt. No soy. No chili. No seasoning of any kind. To eat frog soup, place one frog on your spoon with a little of its broth. Close your eyes, put the frog in your mouth, and bite down. Crunch! Chew well. You eat them bones, guts, eyeballs, and all.

This was our one meal of the day, and it was so wretched that many times I did not want another. And yet living this way was profoundly satisfying. Each dawn we headed into the village for our alms round. The villagers had grown up with this ritual, as had their parents and grandparents. The sun rose and barefoot monks in their orange robes filed out of the forest, cradling their bowls.

We were not allowed to ask for anything. The alms round was accomplished in silence. We walked past the simple huts and the villagers emerged with their offerings. Every morning they began their day with the ritual of monks walking quietly past their homes.

Some rice. Frog soup.

The Buddha said that just like a bird goes from country to country with only the weight of his wings, so a monk goes with only the weight of his robes and bowl. Have you ever seen a bird in the sky carrying suitcases?

The villagers were subsistence farmers. All they farmed was rice. We never had vegetables. There was no fruit. No mangoes. No bananas. We ate rice and whatever crawled or hopped around on the ground. In the wet season there were small, bony fish. Boiled. No salt. No soy.

Through this kind of austerity we learned in our guts what it was to make peace with life. Boiled frog? Good enough. Ant soup? Why not? We took what was given to us and learned to be satisfied. We learned to stop asking for *more*. We learned to stop asking.

We made ourselves easy to look after. The villagers took care of our corporeal needs. And we took care of them spiritually. We chanted for their children when they were still in the womb, gave their kids lessons in being respectful to their parents while encouraging their studies, blessed their marriages and counseled them when they argued, encouraged them to be moral and taught them meditation, looked after them when they became ill, gave them a monastery in which to hang out when they were old, and performed their funeral rites and even chanted in their houses in case they became attached as ghosts. It was literally a service that deserved to be called "before the cradle to beyond the grave."

We were bound together in an ancient dance of giving and receiving. It felt effortless and elemental. The sun came up each morning, and we walked into the village with our bowls in our hands.

It never seemed morally acceptable to me to live at a higher standard than the poorest of our supporters. I was a mendicant, inspired by Saint Francis and his order. I particularly loved the story of Francis's visit to the Vatican to feast with the pope. A couple of hours before he was due to arrive, he went begging in the streets. At the banquet, he shared his scraps with the fat-cat cardinals.

In another inspiring story, a Franciscan monk on his alms round came across a beggar who had absolutely nothing. Not even clothes! The monk gave his robe to the beggar and returned to the monastery naked. When his fellow monks heard what had happened, they thought he was an admirable monk, and he was given another robe from the storeroom.

The next day the monk went out again on his rounds. The local beggars had gotten wind of his generosity. One quickly appeared—naked of course. Presto, the monk's robe was gone and back he went to monastery, where robe number two was replaced.

The third day the same thing happened. This time the monk did not get off so lightly. The abbot summoned him, scolding him at length. "They're taking advantage of you," the abbot shouted. "They think that you're soft in the head!"

The monk didn't try to defend himself, and the abbot finally dismissed him.

Soon there was a gentle knock on the abbot's door. The monk had returned with a cup of hot soup.

"Why have you brought me soup?" said the abbot.

"I thought all that shouting and scolding might have made you hoarse. Take some soup to soothe your throat," the monk replied.

After that the monk could give away as many robes as he wanted. He was beyond teaching as far as the abbot was concerned. The monk's generosity was so selfless that he never even considered his own appearance or comfort, and his compassion for his abbot when being scolded—unfairly scolded, some might say—was singularly awesome. His was obviously so advanced that trying to teach a monk like that would be as pointless as teaching physics to Albert Einstein.

In the time-honored manner, we eat everything out of our alms bowl. There is no course number one and course number two. In goes the curry and in go the sweets. Strawberry ice cream on top of spaghetti Bolognese. I am a master at inventing my own types of fusion cuisine. Quite frankly, I cannot recommend it. I tell myself that it all gets mixed up in the stomach anyway. But going down, it can taste truly grotesque.

I heard about an abbot in England who kept all the leftovers from the day's alms gathering in a large bowl in the freezer. Each morning he had this bowl heated up, adding whatever offerings had come in that day. With a big spoon, he mashed everything together, creating a pungent mush. He'd take whatever was needed for the day and pass it down the line to his monks. He did this for three months, and all his monks disrobed or fled. They couldn't take it anymore!

Alms bowls were traditionally clay, but those disappeared long before my time. My alms bowl, which I received upon my ordination from a sponsor, was iron. I seasoned it in a big bonfire to create a coating of ferric oxide on the outside so it wouldn't rust. There is a special type of leaf in Thailand that when crushed exudes a kind of natural detergent. We used this leaf to clean our bowls.

That wasn't the only plant we used from the forest. Tarzan would have been proud of us! We cared for our teeth with a special type of wood. We cut toothbrush-sized lengths and then smashed the ends with a wooden mallet until they spread out like mushrooms and split the lengths into slivers. The wood tasted slightly bitter and was supposed to have a therapeutic value. We called these slivers "tooth woods." They were a popular offering to our teacher or a senior monk.

We were all malnourished. Many of us became sick because of the bugs. But we survived. The roughness of the life and its hardships did not in any way dilute our happiness. In fact, it enhanced our sense of well-being. We lived so simply, with so little. We always had just barely enough and not a smidgen more. We left what today would be called a "small footprint." We felt almost invisible. Light, airy, and timeless.

It is so very difficult to live simply these days. Our modern age doesn't understand simplicity. The frogs came in season. They lived in the muddy puddles. They weren't factory frogs. They were free-range frogs, organically grown.

7

Giving

EACH DAY AT BODHINYANA, laypeople come and feed us lunch, bringing sumptuous dishes—a grand buffet! They line up before the meal and offer each monk a small spoonful of rice in his alms bowl. This Theravada tradition goes back 2,500 years to the time of the Buddha.

According to our precepts, we can't eat after noon, so the ritual begins around ten thirty in the morning. Forty or fifty people typically show up. Some get up early to cook their finest dishes. Some pick up pizza on the way. Whole families come. It's an outing! Let's go feed those nice monks up in the hills! It is completely uncoordinated, unplanned, and spontaneous. Yet every day the same thing happens—people bring food.

When we first opened our gates long ago, perhaps one or two people would come. Now each day we feast. Why? Why do they come? How is it possible that it happens without any effort, as though it is a natural process, like photosynthesis, the cycle of night and day, the way the rain falls?

There is great joy in giving. Not because someone is rattling a can in front of you. But for the fun of it!

Traveling through the Singapore airport, I saw a woman tossing and turning on a bench. She was obviously trying to get some sleep. A busy stream of passengers rolled by.

I tapped her shoulder. "How about one of these?" I held out my eyeshade.

She smiled, took the shade, gave thanks.

I was high for days on the sweet energy of that exchange.

I learned how much energy we get from giving long ago.

Young men preparing to become novice monks in Wat Pah Pong had to make and dye their own robes. I'd been through that process myself. It was a kind of initiation: a test of your commitment to the path.

You sewed your own robes from white cloth and then the arduous process of dyeing them began. This happened in the dyeing shed. An open-air shack, perhaps six meters square, the dye shed had a corrugated metal roof and wooden benches to either side of an earthen stove, which looked like an Indian tandoori oven that had been made from the dirt shoveled off anthills and compacted and smoothed. A big iron pan sat on top; its bottom was lined with ash so the metal didn't overheat and corrode.

Dyeing involved gathering wood from the forest for your fire and hauling water from the well. You heated the water and added shavings made from branches of the jackfruit tree. You boiled the hell out of those shavings to release the jackfruit sap to make the dye. You had to keep the fire going, concentrate the dye, and infuse the robes with it four or five times to get the proper depth and evenness of color. The dyeing process took days of work, and you had to do it nonstop or the robes would streak, the water would steam off, and the sap would cake. You had to constantly add more water from the well and swish and turn the cloth.

The dye shed also functioned as a laundry. There was no soap in those days. You washed your robes in a weak form of the jackfruit dye.

Our well was fairly shallow, perhaps six meters deep with four meters of water at the bottom. Everyone drank from it. You took your chances with the quality of the water.

We Westerners always seemed to lose the bucket used for drawing water. It was lowered into the well on a long bamboo pole with a hook on the end. After a few buckets had disappeared to the bottom of the well, the main offender (often me) had to fetch a strong rope and be lowered into the well by another monk. I went down into that well many times, an embarrassment more than compensated for by the well's delicious coolness and the opportunity to circumvent the precept against swimming!

During the dyeing of robes, there was no sleep for several brutally hot days and miserably muggy nights.

One evening after meditation and chanting I went to the dye shed. A group of three young monks were in the middle of this grueling process. I remembered my own travails in the dye shed.

"I'll look after the dye pot tonight," I offered. "You go take a rest."

They were off like a flash.

They returned soon after the bell rang at three o'clock. I went to "the morning meeting" where we chanted and meditated. I was surprised: after being up all night I was suffused with energy. The elation lasted through my alms round. I felt so extraordinary that I confessed to my supervising monk that I had broken the rule against helping novices during the dyeing process. "How is it I have so much energy? I haven't slept for thirty-six hours!"

"That's what happens when you help people!" he said.

Isn't it wonderful that what should exhaust and deplete us instead fills us with vitality and joy? When it involves helping people. When it is about *giving*.

When you do something to help somebody, you feel worthy. It generates a feeling of satisfaction and contentment. You savor life rather than fighting it. Life feels replete, overflowing rather than wanting, pinched, and thin.

Giving is a great source of joy. It goes deep into the mind and makes it easier to meditate. To be able to become still you have to be able to sustain attention. There are two ways of doing that. You can force yourself to concentrate. This usually makes you tired and stressed. Or you can develop the perception of joy in whatever it is that you're watching. The beauty in the object holds your attention.

Giving develops a beautiful mind. As you meditate, you're looking at your beautiful mind. You feel a deep satisfaction. You're quite happy to watch it, like a young man transfixed by a beautiful girl. You can't take your eyes off her, and meditating is a breeze!

I had been at Wat Pah Pong with Ajahn Chah for only about two or three weeks and was still learning the routines of a Thai Forest monk's life. Each day at dawn we would all go into the village for our alms rounds. We walked barefoot, and when we returned to the monastery we had to wash our feet before entering the meditation hall.

When Ajahn Chah returned, a posse of monks swarmed him, jostling each other for the chance to bathe his feet. Coming from the West, I thought this highly ridiculous. Water splashed all over the place. Twenty monks madly washed two feet. It was over the top.

My background in science compelled me to investigate this bizarre phenomenon; I would wash Ajahn Chah's feet to see what all the fuss was about. I knew you had to be fast and determined. I arrived early from my alms rounds and took a seat in the washing area, coiled like a cat.

When Ajahn Chah returned, I pounced, diving into the scrum for my master's feet. I got one big toe all to myself. A whole big toe! I was shocked: how happy I felt washing the big toe of an old monk! I realized what all these monks were up to. The pleasure of giving is irrational. But it is real.

I knew a young monk who journeyed from Thailand to see his family in Chicago. Imagine his vertigo. Plucked from the steamy forest of Northeast Thailand and dropped into the brutal Chicago winter.

I suppose the shock was too much for him. He slipped on an icy patch and broke his leg.

Taken by ambulance to the hospital, the leg was soon set. His mother arrived at his bedside. He had never seen her smile as much as she did when she saw him in the hospital bed with his leg in a cast.

He was confounded. "Mom, I'm in pain. Why do you seem delighted?"

"Because now I have you exactly where I want you," she said. "I can mother you, and you can't run away back to Thailand!"

Nothing gives a mother more joy than having a forty-year-old son with a cast on his leg who can't go anywhere and needs to be washed and fed.

For her giving is a privilege—the greatest privilege. The greatest joy. How much happier we would be if we approached life like that mother?

Give, give, and keep giving. And let other people give to you!

8

Hahayana: A Swift Kick in the Ass of Happiness and Wisdom

BOTH VENERABLE GUOJUN and I became Buddhists when we were quite young, and both of us have continued to evolve in our approach to the Dhamma and how we teach.

I became a Buddhist when I was sixteen years old. I was at the Latymer School in London and had gotten my first school prize for what's called A Levels. The prize was enough money to buy one hardcover book. I was concentrating in math at the time and an adviser urged me to buy a book on math. I went to Foyles, a famous bookshop, and the math books looked incredibly boring. I was poor, from a poor family, and there was no way I was going to waste my very hard-earned prize money on equations and theorems. I wanted something weird and dodgy. The esoterica at Foyles was located in the annex on the top floor. That's where I went.

In the annex, I perused books on Buddhism. I looked through Lobsang Rampa's *The Third Eye.* He had pawned himself off as the reincarnation of a Tibetan *rinpoche.* (It turned out that he was actually a plumber, living in

Ireland.) The book itself was wonderfully done. Like Carlos Castaneda, he was both a fantasist and a fantastic author.

I settled on a general book on Buddhism. I liked the fact that in Buddhism there was no God and there was an emphasis on kindness and compassion. The idea of reincarnation also appealed to me. Why should a human existence be perceived like a straight line with a beginning and an end? All that I had studied in science was more like a circle. The earth was a sphere without edges. The universe was curved without any boundaries. Even the seasons turned in a cycle. Why should life be different?

I didn't give a damn what kind of Buddhist I became. It was the early 1970s, and in terms of what was available in Britain at the time I didn't have much of a choice. I attended anything Buddhist. One talk was by a Japanese Zen master. He hardly spoke any English, but I was tremendously impressed by how articulate he was with his limited vocabulary. When somebody asked him his impressions of Buddhism in England, he replied with such eloquence: "Books, books, books! Too many! Dustbin!"

Then came a time when I decided that I wanted to be a monk. It may seem simplistic, but the reason I chose the Thai tradition was because its monks smiled the most. It had nothing to do with philosophy but rather the fact that they were smiling. They were happy. I was drawn to their smiling faces, and that was the beginning of my interest in what I call Hahayana, my vehicle on the Buddhist path.

Not Mahayana, Hinayana, Theravada, Mantrayana. *Hahayana.*

When I started in Buddhism, I wasn't sectarian for the simple reason that in the part of Thailand where Wat Pah Pong was located there were no other sects around! It was very isolated. Later on, when I started traveling, I met monks from other traditions. Now, of course, I travel quite a lot. I stay in other people's temples. We do events together and build up great friendships. Whenever I go visiting friend's temples, it's like my own temple. I don't even see the difference. We just have different robes. The same cake with different icing.

Hahayana expresses the great joy and happiness of the spiritual path. Too long I was told that the spiritual path is dry and intellectual. That wisdom is cold. But I have seen with my own eyes that in the hands of great masters, wisdom is warm and full of humor. It *always* recognizes the primacy of relationships. It seeks to create relationships that are warm, uplifting, and funny! It always insists that it is not about me, not about you: it is always, always, always about *us*.

If religion is the relationship between human beings and the truth, why can't that relationship be funny? Why can't it be fun? The reality is that it is joyful. Fun! And not just an empty fun. Something with meaning to it.

People come to our programs to learn wisdom. They leave happier and wiser.

That can be a simple definition of what love is: the coming together of happiness and wisdom.

Investigate for yourself why that sounds right, and you discover the power of Hahayana.

When I first started teaching the four noble truths in the West, I started out, as you might imagine, with number one: the truth that life is suffering. Most people ran for the doors. They had had enough of suffering in their homes, on the job. No more suffering, *please*, they said. Enough already.

Hm, I thought. Not so effective.

Then, like a good marketer, I thought that I better open by talking about the attractive qualities of the noble truths instead. So I reordered them.

I began with number three, which is usually called "the truth of the end of suffering." What is the end of suffering? It's happiness! When I talked about happiness, people perked up and stayed to listen.

The second noble truth about the cause of suffering then became the cause of happiness. I went on to observe that sometimes, undeniably, we are unhappy— the first truth. Why are we unhappy? I explained that we're unhappy because we're asking something of life that it can't give us. I pointed to the way to resolve this dilemma, the fourth noble truth, the Buddhist path.

I maintain that this was a perfectly legitimate reordering of the four noble truths. That reordering, according to my advertising executive friends, was far more attractive. The same product, repackaged.

In Buddhism it's important to never be attached to one particular path or way of doing things. My disruptive tendencies were instilled early. On the wall of the Department of Physics' Cavendish Laboratory at the University of Cambridge where I was a student, someone had written in graffiti, "The eminence of great scientists is measured by the length of time they stop progress in their field."

When we invest too much in any particular orthodoxy, it stifles our own explorations. Our creativity. Our ability to discover. To play. To have fun!

That was the spirit of Cavendish. I was taught not to be faithful to any particular theory or any school but to always be challenging. Always be changing. Always synthesizing. Moving forward and redefining.

I carried this approach to learning over to Buddhism. I am skeptical of orthodoxies of all kinds.

People say never stand in the shadows of great men. Stand on their shoulders.

I say, no: stand in their shadow, kick their ass, and tell them to get out of the way.

A swift kick in the ass. The coming together of happiness and wisdom. That is the spirit of Hahayana.

The Un*if*able: Make It Right

IT NEVER CEASES to amaze me how much time and energy people spend worrying about decisions. Do I turn left or right? Go here or there? Do this or that?

People come to me all the time and say, "I'm in love, but I can't decide whether or not I should get married."

"The decision to get married is no big deal," I reply. "It's what you do *afterward* that matters."

The bigger the decision, the bigger the worry. So much energy goes into weighing the pros and cons of this possibility or that result. We anticipate the future like fortunetellers with crystal balls. We make decisions as though our happiness hangs in the balance. No wonder that by the time a decision has been made, no energy is left to make whatever it is we have decided on work!

Save your energy for what happens *after* you've made your decision. To make that decision right.

On the question of whether or not to ordain bhikkhunis, I could have chased my tail endlessly around in circles, pondering, "Should I or shouldn't I?" I knew very well that by ordaining them I was going to cause myself a load of trouble. Yet my heart told me that I really had no choice: it was the right thing to do. If it's a choice between your head and heart, always choose your heart.

After you make a choice, the real work starts. Part of that work is resisting the very human temptation to look backward. Don't start thinking "if, if, if": What *if* I had made a different decision? Married a different person? Taken a different job?

We can't know about these ifs. We will never discover what would have happened! Spiritual people like to talk about the ineffable. I prefer the in*if*able.

The past is always inifable. Don't *if* the past. It's a self-inflicted agony and a total waste of time. We will never make peace with life while we dwell on would-have-beens, could-have-beens, and should-have-beens.

Trust your heart when you make decisions. Then spend your energy *making* those decisions right.

Part II.
Flying White

Master Guojun

10

Agarwood: Poison into Beauty

A PRICELESS PIECE of agarwood was my undoing.

Agarwood comes from the infected heartwood of a family of evergreens indigenous to Southeast Asia. The trees produce a dark resin in response to the attack of a certain mold. Agarwood is prized for its fragrance and used in perfume. It also has extraordinary physical properties: the resinous, crystallized heartwood is tremendously hard and dense—so dense, in fact, that it doesn't float. In Middle Eastern desert cultures, it is ground into powder and applied in an aromatic body rub. In Asia, there is a tradition of carving agarwood into sacred objects.

A piece of prized wild (as opposed to cultivated) agarwood fetched an astounding $1,000 per kilo in 2010. The agarwood's value is determined by the age of the tree and the quality and mass of its resinous oil. The original wild population of trees is disappearing, and today agarwood is one of the most valuable natural substances on the planet. And as the wild trees are cut and processed, natural agarwood is becoming increasingly rare.

In 2006 I visited Putian, in southern China, with my close friend and fellow monk Dahui, where I commissioned three statues to be built for the Hall of Universal Light on the main floor of Mahabodhi, the monastery in Singapore that I was in the initial stages of rebuilding. These huge statues, each weighing several tons, were carved to my specifications from solid pieces of white camphor trees that were said to be 1,400 and 2,000 years old. White camphor was chosen not only for its size but because of its other properties: its strong odor repels insects, fungus, and mold, and it has a medicinal quality and a purity and integrity that resists defilement.

It was at the carvers in Putian that I encountered the agarwood—an impressive piece, about seven feet long, three feet high, and eighteen inches thick. It must have weighed over a thousand pounds. I bent down to take a closer look at its intricate carving of deities, many of which I realized I use in my own personal practice.

One such deity, prominently featured, was Mahamayuri Vidyarajni, a bodhisattva who sits on a white peacock. In China, the peacock represents transformation. It eats poisonous insects and worms, and the more poison it ingests, the more lustrous and radiant its plumage becomes. This symbolizes the way we seek to convert the negativity inside us—the three poisons of anger, ignorance, and greed—into something beautiful, beneficial, and pure. The peacock's tail, with its multiple halos, signifies the eyes of the bodhisattva who can see in all directions. The thousand-eyed living embodiment of compassion sees everywhere, even into the darkest and most hidden places, wherever there are sentient beings, in order to help relieve their suffering. Legend has it that Mahamayuri was pursued by hunters who captured him in a net. I recite the mantra that he used to free himself. The net, of course, is the net of suffering in which we are entrapped when we are not mindful.

Also carved into the agarwood was Acala, a wrathful deity with a fierce visage. One of the five wisdom kings, he is another of my personal deities. Acala's wisdom is immovable and unwavering. In one hand he holds a sword that cuts through all defilements; in his other, he wields a rope like a cowboy with a lariat. Our minds are wild horses that need to be lassoed, pacified, and corralled.

A third personal deity featured in the agarwood was Ucchusma, which translates from the Chinese as "unafraid of dirt." He is a manifestation of Shakyamuni Buddha. After Buddha attained enlightenment, the celestials came to pay respects and rejoice—all except one: the Spiral Hair-Knot Brahma King was cavorting with his consorts in his heavenly palace. (A hair knot is twisted, not straight, and represents entanglements.) Outraged that he failed to show Buddha proper respect, the celestials sought to drag the Brahma King out of his heavenly abode. But he made his palace so smelly and foul that no one dared go in. Then, from the Buddha's heart, Ucchusma appeared. Undaunted by the foul odors and filth, he seized the Brahma King and dragged him down to earth to bow at the Buddha's feet.

Dahui could tell I was drawn to the agarwood.

"If you like it, get it for yourself," he said.

"Don't joke! It's much too expensive."

"I know a way," Dahui said. He asked one of his devotees, a businessman who invested in hotels and textiles, and who also knew me and had heard my teachings, to buy it for me to install at Mahabodhi. The businessman was happy to oblige and accumulate the merit that would accrue from such a generous gift. He purchased the piece for about $60,000 Singapore dollars ($30,000–$40,000 US) and donated it to me.

Two years passed, and then in 2008 the work was finally completed in Putian on the camphor Buddhas that would sit in Mahabodhi's main hall. I went to China on a pilgrimage tour with my sangha and asked the manufacturer to send the agarwood to one of my students for safekeeping until the work on the monastery was completed and we could find a suitable place for it. Yet when the monastery was finally finished and the carving was ready to be installed, the ownership of the agarwood was called into question, leading to lawsuits, accusations of financial impropriety, and bogus but nonetheless damaging innuendos of sexual misconduct—which were all widely covered in Singapore's newspapers.

My name and reputation were dragged through the mud, and I have spent countless hours preparing documents and large sums of money on legal fees to defend myself in the courts. In the midst of all this, I left Singapore and traveled through China. I gave serious thought to giving up the abbot's position of Mahabodhi. I even considered disrobing. Members of my sangha persuaded me to come back to Mahabodhi, and, strangely, the whole incident has caused me to renew my bodhisattva vows.

In the beginning of Buddhism, the Buddha established the sangha of monks, nuns, laymen, and laywomen in response to Mara, who acknowledged the Buddha's enlightenment and urged him to depart this world and leave the cycle of birth and death. Mara insisted that the Buddha's work was done. Some sources add that Mara, witnessing the Buddha's enlightenment, admitted that he had been defeated but said he would send his children and grandchildren, disguised as Buddhists, into the sangha to destroy it. The Buddha became quiet and sad—so sad, in fact, that he shed tears. But then he brightened.

"Your descendants will have karmic connections to the Dharma," he told Mara. "You will have sown those seeds into their consciousness. In their future lives, they too will become Buddhist and eventually attain buddhahood!"

Upon hearing this ultimate truth—that our innate goodness and wisdom will eventually triumph—Mara was hopping mad.

The court ruled that the agarwood should be returned to Mahabodhi. I had it installed in the conference room. The agarwood had rapidly appreciated in value and was now worth millions. I have decided to give it to Dahui to sell, to raise money for the charitable work he is doing for children with cleft palates and other congenital disorders in Vietnam.

I have continued my personal practice with the bodhisattva Mahamayuri Vidyrajni, who sits atop a white peacock and freed himself from the hunters' net, and with Ucchusma, who was "unafraid of dirt" and dragged the Spiral Hair-Knot Brahma King out of his filthy abode to bow at the Buddha's feet.

I have come to realize that I need to be like the agarwood. Its special properties are produced when the tree's heartwood is attacked. Life is like that. When you're bitten, stung, or stabbed you secrete substances to protect yourself. It's a natural response. And sometimes this can be a precious thing, *if* we approach this process with the right perspective. Our life experiences sculpt us and make us who we are. This is how we grow, mature, and transform. The peacock spreads his fan. He ingests poison and turns it into luminous halos: our eyes opening to the suffering of others. Falsely accused, branded with depraved behavior and broken vows, I remembered the Dharma of the agarwood. When the tree is attacked, it does not strike out. It turns the poison at its core into something fragrant, precious, and beautiful.

11

Flying White:
Unique and Unrepeatable

I LEARNED the rudiments of calligraphy from my ordination master, Songnian, although he never let me actually draw. I mixed his ink and cut his paper and laid out his tools. He taught me the essence of the art—its spirit. He was considered a national living treasure by the government of Singapore, and his works were much sought after by collectors and connoisseurs. Perhaps if he had lived he would have actually gotten around to teaching me how to put brush to paper. As it was, he died before I made even one stroke. Yet he had planted the seed. When I began the process of rebuilding Mahabodhi in 2009, I wanted to preserve the legacy of Songnian and pass on the lineage, and I was determined to learn calligraphy and carry on the art form that Songnian had mastered and loved.

I took lessons from a calligraphy teacher who had been a good friend of Songnian's. He was an old-fashioned, traditional teacher, strict and very Confucian in his thinking. Calligraphy represented for him a direct connection to tradition that went back thousands of years.

For the first two or three years, his students wrote only their names, nothing more. "How can you do calligraphy if you can't even sign your name?" he told them. He made an exception for me, and I was allowed more freedom of expression.

When I took on the project of rebuilding Mahabodhi, I really didn't know what I was getting myself into. Soon I found myself chasing money, day and night, as the process required it. Since I had some practice in calligraphy under my belt, I decided that perhaps I could raise money in this way. I advertised in a fundraising campaign that I would write sutras in people's names, and these calligraphies would be embedded in the concrete that would make up the building. The whole of Mahabodhi is thus encased with these sutras and the good, supportive energy of the people who sponsored them.

I worked on this project for two years, barely sleeping. It was a marathon. Before the end of the reconstruction, my eyes gave out. It was as though I were looking through a thickening fog that smudged everything and blocked the sun. Sometimes, out of my right eye, it was totally dark. The day before the big Buddha statue was due to be installed in the main hall, I saw an ophthalmologist. He quickly diagnosed a retinal detachment and said I was already three-quarters blind in my right eye. He wanted to operate immediately. I told him he would have to wait until the statue was installed.

He was aghast. "What if you lose the eye?"

"I've waited ten days to see you. I can wait one more. Besides, if I lose the eye, I still have the other," I replied.

While I was doing the calligraphy, copying the mantras and sutras, I realized that each word and every character, even as I repeated them, were not the same. They were always a little bit different. And they were always flawed, always imperfect. As I drew and drew and drew, my writing became smoother. It flowed, but this sense of never quite attaining perfection was always there; it never left. In fact, it became ever more evident. I realized that all the uniqueness and flaws in the characters were actually what made them beautiful, and that connected me to beauty in the uniqueness and imperfections of all the people who were making the donations. Mahabodhi is wrapped in the wisdom of the Dharma, and that Dharma is most powerfully expressed in our fragile and flawed humanity.

This insight into who we are is expressed in a term in calligraphy called *flying white*. It is a deliberate embrace of the imperfection that occurs when the brush does not hold enough ink or pressure and is applied in uneven ways, and there are white areas inside the stroke or at its tailing end. The strokes in calligraphy are a lot like flying—you set out through the air and in one fluid motion come to ground. *Flying white* is a relatively recent development in calligraphy's evolution—it could be thought of as a Romantic school of writing that embraces a kind of spontaneity and emotional force that the classical schools would find too individually expressive.

Flying white points to both our limitations and aspirations. It suggests the ineffable, the transcendent. It is about what is missing. It allows an openness of interpretation, an interaction and connection between the artist and the viewer of the art. It is something that you can't predict—it just happens. It has a kind of freedom. It cannot be practiced. It is like stripes on a tiger's tail. They are never exactly even, never exactly the same. They are the imprint of creation, which always expresses itself in its various forms as something unique and unrepeatable. Those stripes are both dazzling and incomprehensible. I have learned that there's a lot of flying white in both our relationships and our lives.

After the retina surgery, I had two cataract operations. My vision is distorted and blurry. I can't do calligraphy anymore because of my compromised sight. But what I do see is beautiful.

12

Heheyana:
Going beyond Expectations

NOT ONLY are we creatures of habit, we are creatures of expectation. We always have ideas about the way we want life to go. It's the same with spiritual practice. If we want to become enlightened during our practice, enlightenment will inevitably elude us. Our practice will be about the expectation rather than the reality of what is happening in the present moment.

When life does not match our expectations, it's always because we aren't doing what's needed. When we're filled with expectations, positive or negative, it's impossible to be in the here and now and respond appropriately. It's the same with relationships. When we have expectations—projections—in a relationship, we are not really interacting. We are not in the moment, responding to what's being offered, and the situation is compounded if the other person is also operating from a place of expectation! These interactions will be empty of real intimacy, and our expectations will cloud our minds.

And it is the same with our practice. When we live with expectations we are not in the present moment;

we are not living Chan. If you ask a Chan master: "Were you expecting it when you awakened?" the answer will always be "No!" It is always, always, always a complete, total surprise.

To illustrate this point, I tell my students the story of a Chan master who practiced what Ajahn Brahm calls Hahayana and I'll call Heheyana. This master was very short and a little bit fat, with a big round head and sloping shoulders and bushy black eyebrows. He enjoyed making his disciples laugh. He had a thin, high voice, like the whistle of a tea kettle, and his humor was of a very special and disarming type. He was completely deadpan. He never let on when he slipped a joke into his Dharma talks. He would launch into one in the same cadence and tone—and with the same serious, almost hangdog expression—that he used to comment on the sutras, discuss meditation, or talk about anything else that happened to pop into his head.

His jokes were actually funnier because of his stern, foreboding expression. They took his students by surprise, and even when he cracked a joke, it was often unclear to them that it actually was a joke—because after the punch line their master's face would still be as expressionless as a stone.

The students, therefore, could not prepare for the jokes. They could not have that expectation. The jokes came out of nowhere, materializing unexpectedly, almost miraculously. There was never any signal they were coming. But, oh, they were sharp, and their deadpan delivery made them even more devastating.

The students could not contain themselves. They rolled around on the floor. They waved their hands in the air. They tried helplessly to fend off their hilarity. But they could not stop laughing. One burst of laughter led to another and then another, and then when they had finally quieted down someone wouldn't be able to help himself, and he would snicker or snort and then the whole cycle would begin again. And during all of this the master stood pugnaciously at the head of the class, firm on his little feet with his belly sticking out and his foreboding hangdog expression, without even cracking the shadow of a smile. All they needed to do was look at him and they convulsed.

One day, after the master had not cracked a joke for a good long while, he slipped one slyly into his talk about the Sixth Patriarch. Everyone was laughing and laughing—haha, hehe—it was so very, very funny, particularly their little master with his stern, hangdog expression.

Suddenly, while they were laughing, the master shouted, "Who is laughing?!"

In that moment the whole class awakened.

Nothing Special

"What happens when you become a buddha?" one of my students asked me during a recent retreat in Chan Forest, our meditation center in the mountains of Java.

The question took me by surprise, and I laughed. How to respond?

"Nothing special," I finally replied. "Very ordinary. Like you and me."

My students were shocked. So much Buddhism in the East turns Buddha into a deity and places our clergy in a privileged intermediary position between the Buddha's divinity and our flawed humanity. This is not at all the way we understand buddhahood in Chan.

When Buddha awakened under the Bodhi tree, at that moment he realized everyone is Buddha. Buddhahood is nothing special. We are all the same, with the same buddha nature and the same capacity for awakening. It's very ordinary.

My student was quite touched when he heard this answer. He said that I had given him hope. He had felt that as an ordinary person—no one special—it was impossible to achieve the exalted buddha state. It seemed out of reach. Infinitely distant. Like a star.

"The Buddha is a human being," I told him. "Just like you. No difference. There is nothing special about him, nothing supernatural. What he shows us is that through the practice of Chan, all of us, every single one, can awaken. It doesn't matter what race we are, what ethnicity, what gender. Our level of education doesn't matter. How we look—our appearance. Our age. All irrelevant. Attaining buddhahood is all about what we do with our mind, and how we go about living our daily life."

During my court case, I was reminded of my student's question. When I took my seat in the witness stand I felt like I had entered a time machine. Singapore's high court is located downtown, in an ultramodern building. The judge and lawyers wore black robes. The scene looked like something out of a Harry Potter book. People watched the proceedings from behind a glass partition way in the back of the room. As the questioning began, I could feel a very heavy vibe in that room—a thick residue of so many people's anger, frustration, despair, regret, grievance, triumph, vindication, and revenge.

Why does everybody always want to win? I wondered as I sat in the witness stand. Why did that urge seem to overwhelm every other consideration? I thought of my teacher Yin Shun and the institute in Taiwan where I had studied as a young monk. Yin Shun—a pioneer of critical, engaged, leftist, activist, humanistic Buddhism, and one of the foremost scholars of Buddhism of his generation—had helped me see that the Buddha was a man rather than a god. Buddha was born a human being in the human world, and everything he accomplished was in this world, including his passage into nirvana.

We humans are imperfect. The Buddha too! He kept amending his teachings. Even after awakening he needed to try out the teachings and adjust and revise them. It was the *spirit* of the teachings that remained constant. Yin Shun taught us that the Buddha was simply a human being who had reached his full potential. Perhaps most importantly, he made us feel that if the Buddha could do that, we could do it too!

The lawyers spun their web of words, droning on and on. I sat in the hot seat, trying to answer each question as truthfully as I could. There was a sense of unreality. Win or lose—it was only a game, and in the end, I realized, it didn't matter. It was about how you live when you win, or how you live when you lose. How we use our experiences. It is as Ajahn Brahm says: it is not about whether you choose this or that. It's about making that choice right.

Win or lose? Relax. It's nothing special. Very simple; very ordinary.

Let It Come, Let It Go

ALTHOUGH SINGAPORE has over five million people, it is actually a very small island country. The Buddhist community in Singapore is even smaller, tight-knit and gossipy. Everybody is in everybody else's business, and even a whiff of scandal that has to do with a prominent religious figure travels like wildfire.

When the newspapers published innuendo that I was gay, I thought, *Sure, why not?* The following week maybe there would be an innuendo that I liked old women—that I was a lounge lizard—or that I liked young women. Then all women. *Doesn't matter*, I thought, *it's merely words*. Heterosexual, homosexual, bisexual. Whatever sexual. It's okay. No problem. Let it come; let it go.

My students, as you might imagine, did not have quite the same attitude. They were outraged. They felt the lies and innuendos were tarnishing my reputation and undermining the work that I had been doing with their steadfast help and support. I was touched by their loyalty and the strong desire to protect me, although I knew there were limitations to what we could do to. During a retreat in Indonesia, I told them the following story.

There was once a famous Chan master. One day a young woman of aristocratic bearing and appearance brought a baby to the monastery where he was abbot and demanded the monks let her come in.

"Summon the abbot," she ordered. When he appeared before her, she held up the baby. "This is your child," she cried, turning slowly in a circle so that all the other monks who had gathered could see.

It was big monastery, and many monks witnessed this scene. "You have to be responsible," she insisted. The abbot didn't say anything in response. He was very quiet and calm. She thrust the baby toward him. His fellow monks clamored and sought to restrain her.

"Let the child stay," said the abbot. He took the baby in his arms.

The mother turned and fled through the monastery's gate and disappeared.

During the next years, the monk looked after the child, caring for him. The countryside far and wide was rife with gossip about this fledgling who was now being raised in the monastery by an abbot of high repute. The abbot was an object of endless speculation and derision. But he never said anything refuting the claim that the child was his or the multiplying rumors—which had started the moment he accepted the child—that he had many more children scattered throughout the country-side. He looked after the child and went about his work.

The child grew up, well looked after by the abbot and the monks of the monastery, who educated him and taught the Buddhist values of *ahimsa* (nonviolence) and loving-kindness. The child would fall asleep during meditation and services. The monks didn't mind. They just let him be.

Then one day, when the child was seven years old, the monastery was in a state of great alarm. Outside its gates were a thousand soldiers in ranks, bloodstained from a recent battle.

Their leader, a tall young general in full regalia, rode forward from their ranks and commanded the terrified monks to summon the abbot. When the abbot appeared, the general dismounted. Then the woman who all those years ago had left the baby with the abbot came and stood by the general's side. The monks had no idea what was going to happen. Was the abbot going to be beheaded? That seemed the most likely outcome.

Instead, the general and the woman prostrated themselves in front of the abbot, their faces in the dirt. They wept and begged forgiveness. She confessed that the child was not actually the abbot's—it was the young general's. It came out that she and the abbot had been childhood playmates. She was the daughter of a high general who had been a good friend of the monastery's former abbot, and she had grown up playing with that abbot's most gifted and favored monk. The young monk and the girl were very close, very good friends, and the old general had often remarked to the girl that he wished the young man was not a monk so that he could become his son-in-law.

The young woman had fallen in love with her father's aide-de-camp and become pregnant. The couple thought of running away, but they knew the old general would find them and kill them and probably kill the child as well. The old general said he did not want to see the child ever again after it was born.

By this time the old abbot, who was the old general's friend and confidante, had died. The favored disciple and playmate of the young woman became the new abbot. The couple knew the old general would dare not touch the abbot of such an established and highly regarded monastery, particularly because he was so fond of him. So they hatched a plan to leave the child at the monastery for safekeeping.

Now, they said through their tears, the old general had died in battle and the child's father had been promoted to the supreme rank by the emperor. They had come to reclaim their child.

The abbot listened in calm silence to this account. When it concluded, he said, "Bring the boy."

"These are your real parents," he told the boy. "Now it is time for you to return to them and assume your place in the world." In China, children have no say. He might have wanted to stay with the monks. Who knows? For his part, the abbot was full of compassion. The abbot hugged the boy, and then he turned and went back into the monastery and on with his work.

15

Cultivating the Mind-Field

CHINESE MONKS wear pants because traditionally we
had to work on farms. The monasteries were usually out
in the countryside, and the monks grew their own food.
We have an expression in Chan, *nong chan*, which means
"farming meditation." The texts in our tradition that use
the language of "cultivation" and "mind-field" reflect
the way farming is interwoven in our tradition. Plow to
remove stones, loosen up soil, sow seeds, and cover them
with earth; water, fertilize, weed, thin, pick! During these
tasks monks were taught to be mindful and aware. The
rhythmic nature of the work—repetitive actions, done
in silence—was the nong chan practice. The monks
learned not to ask why they had to farm. They grew food
so they could eat. They were farmers in order to survive.
Similarly, they meditated both in the fields and on the
cushion for their spiritual life to survive and flourish.

I got a taste of this practice when I trained in Taiwan's
Fu Yan Institute in Hsinchu. You could say the institute
was a college, except that its students did the cooking
and cleaning. About one hundred of us were enrolled
when I was there. We farmed a small area of land for

food. In winter we chopped firewood to heat water for our showers. We washed our own clothes—a habit I retain to this day—and we handled carpentry, electrical, plumbing, and general maintenance.

We woke at three or four, depending on the schedule for our early morning duties. We slept in bunks, six or eight to a room. We learned basic Buddhist ceremonies and rituals. We read *The Way to Buddhahood* and studied the Pure Land school, bodhisattva precepts, and Nagarjuna's commentary on the *Mahaprajnaparamita Sutra*. We read the Tiantai and Vipassana commentaries and the Agama sutras. We studied the histories of Indian and Chinese Buddhism and their major texts. There were seminars where we delivered papers. It was solid, basic Buddhist education.

I had to work quite hard. I always skipped dinner, keeping a small bun that we had for lunch and eating that. My companion was the Dharma, the teachings. They kept me company. It was a pure life. Very simple. I worked the institute's small plot of land. We grew sweet potato greens, a hardy crop of nondescript taste that didn't need much looking after and was quite nutritious. We also grew cabbage, spinach, and bok choy. It was in these first tentative forays into nong chan that I began to develop an awareness of the mindfulness practice that I still teach today: wherever the body is, the mind is there; whatever the body is doing, the mind is doing it too. Mind and body, in harmony together.

Nong chan teaches us to cultivate the plants with a unified mind—we are one with the crops and the elements and our labor or activity, which is the source and sustenance of our lives. The growing process can't be rushed, and each plant is different. We need to appreciate it on its own terms in order for it to flourish. It is the same when we're in the Chan hall—we are all different and ripen at our own pace and in our own way.

Chan has been called "a special transmission outside the scriptures, not founded upon words and letters." Nong chan grounds us in activity that is about an intuitive awareness that has nothing to do with words. It is about losing yourself in the elements: sun, water, wind, earth. Rather than think, *I need to water the crops*, nong chan tells us to think, *The crops need water*. Rather than focusing on our own needs and desires, we learn to simply respond to what's needed. We are not separate from the rest of humanity, from the earth itself.

As I practiced nong chan, I felt as though I were going back to the source, to the beginnings of Chan, to the place where my life began. I saw our practice extending through generations of great teachers who had cultivated cabbages in the mind-field and realized themselves, passing along the teachings to us through the tunnel of time.

16

Crossing the River, Smelling Fish

ONE DAY my master Sheng Yen and I were walking through the forest at his retreat center in Pine Bush, upstate New York. It was spring and there had been snowmelt and lots of rain. A normally placid stream that was easily crossed had turned into a raging torrent.

"Do you think the river god will open up this stream for us so we can walk across?" Sheng Yen asked.

"Shifu, let's leap over!" It was a beautiful spring day, and I was a young, impetuous monk who thought I could do anything. I knew Sheng Yen enjoyed this aspect of my character, so I was free with my words. "Keep your impulsive energy and turn it into *bodhichitta*," he would tell me. Bodhichitta is the motivation to awaken all sentient beings.

We studied the muddy, rushing stream. "The bodhisattva path is not as easy as you think," Sheng Yen said. There was a wistfulness about him—a sadness. The retreat center was experiencing a lot of difficulties, and I felt the weight of these problems as he told me the following story, which perhaps was a Buddhist folktale that he had heard when he was a child.

There was once a Brahman arhat who every day went to hear Buddha teach. On his way, he had to cross a river and so he'd call out to the river god, "Babu, open up! I want to walk over." The river god paid respects to the arhat, and the arhat likewise paid respects to the river god, and the river god opened a way for the arhat to walk through. The arhat went to see the Buddha and then returned home, again exchanging greetings with the river god, who opened a path through the flow.

This ritual went on day after day, the same exchange of words over and over, until one day when the river god became upset and went to complain to the Buddha. "He keeps calling me *Babu*," said the river god. *Babu* is how you address a servant, someone low class and insignificant.

The Buddha asked the arhat to meet with the river god. "Have you been respectful to the river spirit? Have you looked down on him?" the Buddha asked the arhat.

"That wasn't my intention," said the arhat. "If I made him feel that way, I'm very sorry for it, and I apologize."

"You see?" the Buddha said to the river god. "He apologized to you and he is sincere. It is just his habit, as he is from the Brahman caste," the Buddha said.

After he finished telling the story, Sheng Yen said, "I don't think the river god will help us today." We returned to the retreat center.

Several days later, Sheng Yen took up this theme of the way our habits shape our behavior during a Dharma talk in the Chan hall. He told a story about Ananda.

One day the Buddha was taking a walk with Ananda in the marketplace. The market was done for the day—the vendors had left and the stalls were empty. The Buddha saw some discarded banana leaves, which the vendors had used to wrap up their goods, on the market floor. The Buddha asked Ananda to pick one up and inspect it.

"Can you see anything inside the leaf?" the Buddha asked.

"No," Ananda replied.

"What do you smell?"

"Salted fish." Ananda picked up another leaf. "Jasmine flower," he said.

"What does this mean?" the Buddha asked.

Ananda, as usual, was perplexed.

"You cannot see the fish or the flowers," the Buddha explained. "But you can smell the things that are left over, the residual."

Sheng Yen used the word *xi qi* in Chinese to refer to these residuals. *Xi qi* can be translated as "smell habit," but *qi* also means energy. Sheng Yen was drawing from the complex matrix of Buddhist philosophical teaching on intention and karma, and he was pushing us as his students to carefully investigate our own habits and suppositions.

Karma is a type of energy. We cannot conceive of

karma: it's too complicated. An analogy might be a seed from a mango. It drops and produces a mango tree. Three years later that mango tree produces one hundred mangoes, which all drop and produce trees that also bear fruit and then produce a thousand trees, and so on. One seed or one very small action can produce a vast multiplicity of effects. The Mahayana view is that even though I may not have had the intention to disrespect or harm you, if I do, then I have created karma. With the right view, we can see many of the problems in our relationships and the world from this perspective.

As Sheng Yen told this story, I again sensed the wistfulness in him that I had felt when we were together by the rushing stream.

"We all still have lots of habits; we are imperfect, and we should not take things too hard," Sheng Yen said. He looked at me. His eyes were sad with a kind of helplessness. I thought he would go on and say more. But he simply said, "That's all for tonight," and he rose from the *pu tuan* (cushion) on which he sat and walked slowly into the dark passage behind the dais.

These stories have recently returned to me as I have been in the midst of my own troubles. Sheng Yen was cautioning us against judging the actions of others. He was saying that very often our habitual tendencies produce unintentional effects, and that we have to be mindful of this in our relationships. The subtle but powerful filter of *xi qi* is pervasive.

I have often thought of the way Sheng Yen looked at

me that night in the Chan hall. The feeling was more than an older man to a younger man, more even than master to disciple. It was the way a father might look at a son. In the midst of his own troubles and challenges, he knew that I would face difficulties too—that they were inevitable, and there was nothing he could do to prevent what was coming.

I want to tell him now, as I write this, that I am okay. The energy for bodhichitta is still there inside me. I feel it moving, welling over. And I will never give it up.

17

Embrace Uncertainty

I HAVE ALWAYS been drawn to what some people would consider extreme activities. I like to test my limits and have an adventure. I'm not necessarily drawn to activities that are dangerous, but I've always been attracted to those things that prompt us to see our real selves, beyond the masks we wear, that put us up against who we really are.

In my younger days as a monk I tried bungee jumping in northern Thailand. I took a slow lift, the kind you see at construction sites that are used on skyscrapers, which was attached to the face of the cliff and ascended to its lip. When I got to the top and looked down, my heart began racing. On the edge of the lift was a metal extension, a catwalk that stretched out. Below was a largish pond.

My legs and lower body were tied with Velcro straps and thick belts. I hopped out on the metal catwalk. My knees were wobbly, and I began to shake. It was like walking the plank or going off a high diving board, except that it was much, much higher. The water glistened below me. I felt weak. Apparently this moment is too much for some people. They start weeping and refuse to jump.

I was fascinated by the moment at the edge, right before you leap. I knew that I wasn't in any danger. And yet the fear was overwhelming on the first jump. You have that fear even though you *know* nothing bad is going to happen. It teaches you that there is a deep divide between knowing something with your mind and experiencing it. You might say the moment of jumping, of hurling yourself into space, is a breakthrough. *Just do it*, you tell yourself. Once you step over the edge there is no going back. You have done something incontrovertible. In free fall, nothing is solid and there is nothing to hold on to. There is no way to control the experience. You have to surrender, and with that surrender comes the taste of liberation.

The taste is like the shadow of a bird. It has similarities to, although it is not the same as, an enlightenment experience that Sheng Yen has described. As a young monk he shared a room one night by chance with Grandmaster Ling Yuan, a famous Chan monk. They sat on a large raised platform that is traditionally where Chinese people sleep. Sheng Yen was excited to be in the company of such a renowned monk, and he began asking him many questions. Sheng Yen said these were questions that had been plaguing him about Buddhadharma, and that at this point in his development he was full of doubt. Ling Yuan didn't respond except to say, "Any more? Any more? Any more?"

It grew later and later and Sheng Yen said he felt a

sense of desperation verging on panic. Would his questions never be answered? Was he doomed to a life of gnawing doubt? He asked the next question, and out of nowhere the monk slapped his hand to the platform and shouted, "Put it down!" At that moment, Sheng Yen said, he had an awakening.

Put it down! When you're in free fall, that's all you can do. Unfortunately, it's extremely unlikely that we'll become enlightened bouncing around on the bungee cord.

Skydiving, another activity I tried, has many of the same qualities as bungee jumping. When you're in free fall, hurtling toward the earth, the only thing you can control is your mind. You have to be free of resistance to what's happening. You have to be totally open. You need to go with the flow, a lesson we have to relearn over and over.

Another extreme activity I did had opposite qualities. In bungee jumping and skydiving you want to slow down your experience, but when you're scuba diving, you often want to get back to the surface as fast as possible!

I went diving to attain great depths off the Great Barrier Reef in Australia. You have to descend slowly and come up slowly, being careful to give your body time to adjust to the change in pressure. The bends can kill you, and there is a strict protocol that must be followed. You can't rush it.

As you descend, you feel a building intensity of fear. The sun is overhead, growing ever more faint. The sky becomes a distant memory. The darkness envelops you, and the water grows cold. You must relax. As you go farther and farther into the dark, your imagination runs wild. Are there monsters lurking beyond your ever-decreasing field of vision, horrible things with fangs waiting to devour you? There is less and less life in the gloomy depths, but the fish increase in size. And they're not the colorful fish of the reefs anymore; they're big fish in drab shades of black and brown. It's important to regulate your breath—you have to conserve your air. You must remain calm, descending at a measured rate and stopping often to adjust to the increasing pressure.

During the dives, I learned how we fear the unknown, and how even in the face of this fear we need to have a relaxed awareness. When we do this we are able to discover ourselves. The deeper that I went into the ocean, the deeper I felt I was going into myself. At the dive's nadir the only illumination was from a small headlamp I wore. No matter how spooked I was, I had to make sure my ascent was done slowly and deliberately.

The experiences of free fall and diving to great depths teach us to not grasp at the way we want things to be. We must accept the pace of the experience. Difficulties will end when they end. Not knowing makes us fearful, but life is filled with uncertainty. It is far better to embrace this fluidity than to resist it or pretend that our lives and the lives of those we love won't pass away.

Our recourse is to keep coming back to the present moment. As you jump, there is no feeling of "why me?" and no sense of right and wrong. In the depths, we begin to see where our fears of the unknown originate. We emerge from the void, and it is to the void we return. There is no point in resisting. Falling through space and gently breathing in the abyss—these experiences are great teachers.

Sky Poem III

We want forever
but we are not

Carried for eons
on our shoulders
nobody else did this to us
we to ourselves

Nothing extraordinary
nothing exceptional
nothing supernatural
it's okay
no big deal

Eyes looking for eyes
head looking for head
all of it
always with you
simple
direct
beautiful

Untainted
like the sky
without plus or minus
completely
zero

Grateful grateful grateful
Buddha raga
for everything that is

Put it down
a thousand tons

Hit bash kick kill
doesn't matter

Each moment *alive*
that is
our true nature

19

The Seven Wonders of Chan: Right Here, Right Now

WE USUALLY DON'T realize the preciousness of the breath. We breathe in; we breathe out. Nothing special. It is always helpful to remind ourselves that the breath is precious. Try this experiment: Cover your mouth with one hand and plug up your nose with the thumb and index finger of your other hand. Stop your breath for as long as you can. When you feel as though you're suffocating, release your hands and breathe. How do you feel?

It is so good to be breathing. Why don't we feel that way most of the time? The breath is so precious. We generally walk around disconnected from the breath because we lack awareness. How much richer our lives would be if we really felt our breath and appreciated it. When we feel the breath, we feel our lives. We feel the goodness of life. We feel that this life is precious and wonderful.

We could think of this appreciation of the breath as the first of the seven great wonders of Chan. What were the seven wonders of the ancient world? The Great Pyramid of Giza in Egypt. The Colossus of Rhodes. The

Hanging Gardens of Babylon. The Lighthouse of Alexandria. The Mausoleum at Halicarnassus. The Statue of Zeus at Olympia. The Temple of Artemis at Ephesus.

Our Chan wonders are infinitely grander! The first wonder of Chan is the breath—to be able to breathe. The second is our sight—we are able to see. The third is our hearing. The fourth is to be able to taste. The fifth is to be able to talk, communicate, and sing. The sixth is our ability to use our bodies: to move, act, walk, dance, run, hug, touch! And the seventh wonder is that we can think, we have a mental functioning. These are the great wonders of Chan.

When we're in the midst of hardship and difficulty, we can come back to these wonders. First and foremost, we can come back to the breath. We can focus our awareness on the way that the breath waits for no one. It just keeps coming and going, coming and going. It will not stop for you. Just like the river will not stop—it flows and flows, it doesn't wait—so it is with our lives. They just keep going. They keep moving forward. Each moment is gone and will never return. And then another new moment will come. When we have this awareness, it inspires us to do everything wholeheartedly. We don't get caught in worry or regret. We come back to the breath. To our moment-to-moment experience.

We can always embark on a grand tour of Chan's seven wonders—first class and all inclusive! We don't have to go anywhere to experience them! They are completely available. They are always with us. Right here, right now.

20

Many Dishes Make a Meal

I MADE A VOW to my ordination master, Songnian, that I would rebuild Mahabodhi monastery after his passing on. I have done that. It's a beautiful building. Every detail reflects the Dharma, and our calendar is packed with programs organized by our sangha.

The way the monastery is structured represents the interwoven strands of my own practice. Upstairs on the third floor is a Chan hall for sitting meditation. The second floor has a tantra hall for rituals that have to do with the Mantrayana Buddhism that I have been studying in Taiwan. The main hall is designed after the Xian Shou school of Chinese Buddhism—another of the lineages in which I have received transmission—which is largely based on the *Avatamsaka Sutra*. This sutra is about the interdependence and inter-being of all things.

Chinese Buddhism is unique in this way; it has a tradition of combining and blending different Buddhist schools, and it embodies the cultural diversity of China. It is a lot like the way we eat in China. Lots of small plates, which everyone shares. A little bit from here, a little bit from there. A harmonious combination of different flavors. There is no "main course."

In Chinese food we balance different tastes: sour, sweet, spicy, bitter, salty, and plain. We like our cooking to reflect life itself! Life is never easy—it has all these flavors. Most of us will have the full range of experiences.

Our experience is always relative. When you taste a spoonful of honey and then bite into an apple, what do you taste? Sour. When you suck on a lemon and then have a bite of the same apple, how does it taste? Sweet!

Sweet, sour, spicy, salty, bitter, plain. Many dishes make a meal. Missing any of these flavors—even the bitter or sour—diminishes life. Life that is always sweet is not real life. We want to taste all of life's different flavors, no matter if sometimes they are difficult to swallow.

21

Just Let It Be

WHEN WE ARE truly in the present moment, we experience what in English is called *equanimity*. This English term is associated with a feeling of imperturbability. Whatever happens, happens, and we maintain a feeling of calm composure. There is a sense of detachment, of being peacefully uninvolved, of letting whatever comes come and whatever goes go. Equanimity is associated with being on an even keel, and it is certainly something most people value, but not in quite the same way as it is valued in Buddhism.

In Sanskrit, equanimity is *upeksha*; it is one of the *brahmaviharas*, or four immeasurables, along with loving-kindness, compassion, and appreciative joy. Why is equanimity such a big deal? It is because it brings us to a realization of our nondiscriminating mind, into a place of nonattachment and nonduality, where differences are resolved between this and that, here and there, right and wrong, inside and outside, you and me. Everything is equal.

In fact, there is no difference between thoughts. There is only one thought. The thought is the present moment, without past or future. There is no conflict, no opposition, no contradiction, and we have a deep sense of peace, serenity, and tranquility. Everything seems to be very still and very settled. Equanimity means to be totally relaxed, totally and absolutely. There is nothing to worry about. Everything feels easily and comfortably arranged. Each tree in the forest is placed just so. Each leaf on each tree is exactly where it should be. And so it is with the rocks, and the fields and the rivers. Everything is just right as it is. There is no need to add or subtract. Just sit, just stand, just walk, just drink, just eat, just sleep. The wind blows and the thunder roars and the rain falls. Just let it be.

In the *Lotus Sutra*, we see the verse "All phenomena abide in their position." In Chinese we render this phrase *Fa zu fa wei, se cien xia chang zu.* It means everything is nicely set. The right thing appears in the right place at the right time. It's a little bit Daoist—everything in harmony, a balance in nature of which the human world is also part. Let nature take its course. Everything will fall into place by itself. There is no need to grasp, reject, or repulse, and we have a feeling of liberation. A load of bricks has been lifted from our shoulders that we didn't even know we were carrying.

The world is perfect as it is. Down to the smallest, most insignificant detail. The ant crawling across the floor. The spider hanging on the tree. The birds flying. Just let it be. Relax. Relax totally and completely. There is no need to do anything. Whatever we have been search-

ing for, whatever we have been striving for—all unnec-
essary! Equanimity means that we discover something
immeasurable that we have never actually lost.

22

Bonsai: Provoking Growth

WHEN I CAME to live at Mahabodhi it was a modest dwelling, a two-story bungalow that had been converted into a monastery from a private residence. The huge Daoist temple that now sits next to it was originally a small hut. The apartment complex across the way, fifteen-story buildings that house thousands, was just a grassy hill.

Songnian liked the fresh air and being close to nature in this sleepy, rural part of Singapore. He was worlds away from the refined milieu in which he had grown up.

He was sick in childhood. I imagine him living in a big house with courtyards and gardens. I think he may have been lonely. He spent his days learning calligraphy, painting, and poetry, and reading the Chinese classics. I don't think he was close to his parents. It's not clear why he became a monk—maybe it was because he was sickly? The traditional Chinese understanding is that when one is sick and can't do much, perhaps it is better to go into a monastery, to cloister oneself away from the stresses and strains and aspirations and ambitions of the world.

Like thousands of other Chinese Buddhist monks, he had fled the mainland in 1949 when the Maoists seized power. He took refuge in Hong Kong's Deer Garden Temple, and he thought about what to do next. The Chinese diaspora is strong throughout Asia, and wherever the Chinese have gone they have carried their own particular forms of Mahayana Buddhism with them, even in countries in Southeast Asia with strong Theravada traditions. For over a decade, Songnian roamed through a network of temples, monasteries, and Buddhist institutes that taught Dharma not only in Hong Kong and Taiwan but also Malaysia. He studied Buddhism in the Cameron Highlands and spent three years on retreat in San Bao Cave. His health was not good, he didn't like the cold, and that may be one of the reasons he came to Singapore in 1960. He assumed the abbotship of Mahabodhi in 1963 and spent the last thirty-four years of his life there.

Songnian taught calligraphy and drawing and religious ritual and instruction to Singapore's monastic community. His standards were very high, and he eventually gave up religious instruction. He decried the lack of culture and art in the Singapore of his day. His health was often bad and that stopped him from being too active, which was his main regret. He often said that he would have liked to have led retreats to spread Buddhadharma.

Songnian spent much of his time in the contemplative pursuits of a cultured Chinese gentleman. One of these was bonsai. Dozens upon dozens of these dwarf-like trees sat on metal shelves in the courtyard behind the gate to either side of Mahabodhi's entrance. This was Songnian's miniature forest. The bonsai required careful, constant care.

He never allowed me to do anything that had to do with the actual shaping of the tree. "You're much too clumsy and stupid for the bonsai," he would say. Everything with the bonsai had to be exact. If a leaf turned yellow or fell he would scold me: "Seeds for Hell, see what you've done!"

Seeds for Hell was his nickname for me, and I often wondered at its meaning. Why Seeds *for* Hell? Seeds *of* Hell would have made more sense. Regardless, what was clear was that he was insulting me, although even at my young age with my limited understanding I knew that his constant barrage of derision and criticism was part of my training. We lived together and I served him and that was the way he taught me. There were no Dharma talks or heart-to-hearts with my master. His teachings were as constant and unrelenting as his attainment. Perhaps I romanticize. Perhaps what was really going on was that he was simply a grumpy old man in ill health who was fed up with life and frustrated by being surrounded by mediocrity. I suppose there is truth in that view. But like so much of life, it was both this and that. Songnian's lessons could be harsh, but now I see they prepared me for the challenges I would one day face. Seeds for Hell was prescient. It anticipated a dark flowering.

The bonsai had to be watered two or three times each day. I must say I was surprised when Songnian told me to do this. He let me water in the Chinese way: terrible equipment, high degree of skill. I had to turn on the tap to a basic garden hose at just the right pressure and precisely position my fingers over the spout to create the perfect mist.

Songnian would inspect the plants and the stone patio underneath them when I was done. He could gauge how much water I had used and whether or not I had been able to achieve the proper density and duration of the spray. There was never any verbal instruction. I had to watch him and carefully observe. He didn't say what was right, only what was wrong. I learned that too much water would make the soil run away and too little would mean the tree could not absorb enough moisture.

Sometimes we repotted the plants. It was a delicate operation, requiring great care not to damage the roots. I stood at Songnian's side, handing him his tools, which were like regular tools for horticulture except much smaller. He worked with special wires to bend the branches of his trees, shaping each one to something growing in his mind. He was very quiet, totally absorbed. His movements were delicate and refined. A feeling of peace and gentle concentration guided our work. The bonsai were living sculptures molded by his hands.

The area outside the monastery where Songnian cultivated his bonsai was very neat and tidy. There was not a speck of soil on the ground. No sloppiness. The bonsai were a mindfulness practice for him. He nurtured the bonsai in the same way he cultivated the Dharma.

The green colored wires we used to shape the bonsai had to be attached with extreme finesse in order not to scar or wound the fragile bark. The duration that the wires were affixed was also exacting. If left too long, the bark would grow around the wire, which meant the wire couldn't be removed without damaging the bark. If attached for too short a period, the limb would not bend sufficiently to the vision in Songnian's mind.

As a young monk, I felt the artistry in the bonsai. They were so refined. So detailed. Songnian cultivated them in a way that made me feel they were ancient. Gnarled roots breached the soil, pointing to the depth and breadth of the tree's foundation. You could feel the bonsai's stability, its grounding. They evoked ancient giants scaled way down.

As we moved among the miniature trees, Songnian would occasionally talk about the Huangshan mountain range in southern Anhui province. Huangshan was a favorite landscape for traditional Chinese painting: soaring cliffs, deep ravines, and cloud-shrouded escarpments. The painting might have a small hut and a human figure somewhere in the scene. The human presence was typically tiny, insignificant, overshadowed by the majesty of nature. The traditional paintings were vertically composed. Mountains ascended into the clouds, piercing *tian*, heaven, the celestial realm.

In my impressionable mind, Songnian's words conjured another dimension where the immortals, like fairies, flitted through the clouds. He would talk about how lovely that landscape was, and how the bonsai evoked those forests for him. He walked slowly, almost majestically, through the shelves of trees, breathing them in one by one, over ground that I had swept spotless. He wandered through his ancient groves, consorting with immortals.

Songnian said to me more than once: "Plants are better than humans. If you take care of the plant, it will flourish. Its leaves shine. Not human beings. Take care of them and what do you see in return? Nothing." And then he would turn his eyes toward me, the long bristles of his lashes curving downward, fixing me with his hawk-like gaze. "You are worse than the bonsai," he said. I was completely baffled. What in the world did he mean?

Sometimes he would make me pluck all the leaves from the water jasmine bonsai. He called this "shaving the head" of the trees. I always felt this was an almost violent act—the trees looked denuded, fragile, close to death. Yet after we plucked the leaves the tiny trees would bloom with a profusion of delicate white flowers. These star-like blooms emitted a sweet-spicy jasmine fragrance that perfumed the air. Songnian would be pleased. I knew that he was teaching me. This stripping down, the merciless plucking, was what caused the bonsai to bloom. When we are completely shaken, totally shattered, it can provoke new growth. A blossoming that is fragrant and beautiful.

23

Just Is Just Just

WHEN WE TRULY RELAX, we are preparing ourselves or training ourselves to resonate with a state of what we call justness. And what is just? Just is just just. Just this. Not too much. Not too little.

In Chinese Buddhist sutras, the verses open with the words *ru shi*, or *thus*. *Ru* has many meanings. It can mean "if" or "or." But it is also the yin character for woman, the feminine, for feminine ways of feeling and creating. The second character, *shi*, means "is" or "real." It is composed of two parts: on top is the character for the sun, and below is the character for a man walking. When you're walking under the sun, everything is clear.

Ru shi is followed by *Wo wen*. The sutras repeat this opening phrase over and over. *Ru shi wo wen. Wo* is "I." *Wen* is composed of the character of an ear inside a door.

We can translate this opening phrase as "thus I have heard" or "as it is." In other words, these are the original words as heard from the Buddha. The relationship between the person reading or reciting and the writer is one of accord and repetition.

There is no sense of judgment in *ru shi wo wen*. We should not translate it as "I have listened," because *listened* implies more than simply hearing. It implies judgment or understanding. Our ego, that sense of "I," is involved.

Justness. As it is. Thus I have heard. These expressions point to an acceptance of what is. It has always been thus. It has always been as it is. It is just this. No more, no less. Why didn't we realize it earlier?

Our true nature is never about right or wrong. It is about being at peace with what is. It is about loving all of it. When we want things to be better than they are, we're not staying in the present moment. As Ajahn Brahm says, we're asking something of life that it can't give us. What is right here right now is already the best. This is why Chan can be thought of as a kind of ultimate realism. Our response to life should never be one of disappointment. What we need to do is make the most out of each moment and live our lives to the fullest. That is really what Chan teaches us.

Just is just just. Suchness is such—no more or less. Thus! These words point to a meaning beyond meaning. They are almost nonverbal. They are a shout or cry, an eruption of pure being. They are nonrhetorical and precognitive. They point to nonthinking. They are emphatically as they are. As it is.

24

Seeds for Hell: Seeing Under
the Surface of Things

SIX MONTHS AFTER I came to Mahabodhi and Songnian shaved my head, he became ill.

It began as a slight pain after breakfast. He thought it was indigestion and berated the nuns who cooked for him: "Look what you've done to my stomach! What poison did you feed me?"

The pain rapidly worsened. By midmorning it was acute. The family doctor arrived, examined Songnian, diagnosed appendicitis, and said that we needed to get him to the hospital. Songnian was barely able to speak through clenched teeth, but he made it quite clear that he did not want to be hospitalized.

"If the appendix ruptures, he could die," said the doctor.

I don't know where I found the strength, but I picked Songnian up and draped him over my back. He cursed me: "Seeds for Hell, you want me dead," he hissed. "You are trying to murder me."

I trotted out Mahabodhi's front door, carrying Songnian piggyback as fast as I could to the doctor's car. I pushed him into his seat as he repeatedly cursed me and called me a murderer. As we drove to the ER, he was in too much pain to do anything but gasp, hiss, and cry out. At the ER he was immediately wheeled into surgery. They opened him up to remove his appendix, which, as it turned out, was just fine. He had been misdiagnosed! It turned out that the problem was gallstones. A second incision was made and eighteen stones removed.

To say Songnian was displeased that he had two painful incisions rather than one is putting it mildly. During the first days of his convalescence he was furious and refused to talk to me. When he finally did begin talking, he again accused me of trying to kill him.

"Seeds for Hell, you want me to die because I've been too tough on you," he said. "You resent your training. You hate me, and you want to take revenge and do away with me. Your plan is to kill the old monk and become abbot!"

This line of attack was completely unexpected and stunned me. "Shifu, it wasn't me that wanted you to come to the hospital. It was the doctor. He said you must come in. It was an emergency. We wanted to save you so that you will have a long life."

Then, inexplicably, he grinned. "What's the point of living so long? Can't you see that I've lived enough? Do you think that I'm greedy for life? Is that your idea? I've done enough. It's time for the younger generation to take over. It's your turn now!"

We went through this baffling routine a number of

times. No matter what I said, he contradicted it. Everything was up in the air, being flipped around and reversed on a whim.

I stayed by Songnian's side in the hospital night and day, sleeping in a chair in his room. Sometimes he would wake and call for me to fetch his prayer beads or bring him water. He was unfailingly polite and cooperative with the doctors and nurses. A real pussycat. But as soon as they left the room, he was fierce. "You're trying to kill me," he insisted. "You want the old fellow dead. You're licking your chops. You want to murder me so you can take over and become abbot!"

I tried not responding. I thought that if I gave his anger free rein it might burn itself out. Fat chance!

"Seeds for Hell! Are you deaf? Am I talking to a block of wood? A stone? Are you awake? Or asleep?"

He had a sharp tongue even in his weakened state.

I often did feel as though I were half asleep after many nights in the hospital chair and many days that were spent waiting on him. I was dead on my feet. A zombie. And his words bounced off me.

Instead of arguing with the accusation that I was trying to murder him, I thought it might be a better tactic to just agree with whatever he said.

"Yes, Shifu," I said, bowing and bowing.

"*Yes, Shifu*." He mimicked me in a prissy, mocking voice. "*Yes, Shifu*. Seeds for Hell! That's all you know."

Songnian had been strong and vigorous before the operation; afterward he wasted away. He began to steadily lose weight and he became increasingly inward and inert. He was wheelchair-bound and refused to wear diapers. This often meant we didn't get him to the bathroom in time and he would shit himself.

It was my job to clean him after these incidents, helping him up from the chair, supporting him in the shower, and gently and carefully washing the excrement from his body. Most of the time, however, he screamed at me that the water was either too hot or cold. "Are you trying to boil me alive?" he hissed. "Do you want me to freeze to death?"

I came to recognize that this was not the kind of purely contrary, oppositional behavior you might encounter in a child. There *was* a correct water temperature, which I could deduce from the weather, the time of day, and how active Songnian had been. He was teaching me to see under the surface of things. To be flexible and constantly adjust to circumstances and not to be entangled in any one fixed approach or method. This was very Chan. To trust in another kind of knowing and doing—the method of no method.

After I bathed him, I carefully dried him off with a towel. If I rubbed too hard, he screamed at me: "*Bapi!*" which could translate as "You're skinning me alive!" When he gauged my touch too soft, he accused me of purposefully leaving him wet so he would catch a chill. "I know your tricks. You plan to give me pneumonia and watch me die a slow and terrible death!" he said.

Occasionally, when I anticipated a tongue lashing, he sighed with contentment as I dried him off and thanked me for cleaning and bathing him, calling me a bodhi-sattva! It was impossible to know what to expect.

He refused to let me sleep in his room at night. "You plan to murder me and steal my things," he insisted. He distrusted banks and kept all the money he had received from *dana* offerings in his cupboards and in ancient suit-cases under his bed.

I slept outside his door on a mat. When he needed me, he pressed a button and a bell rang. I dragged myself awake, stumbling into his room, drained after a long day of dogged service: cleaning, sweeping, mopping, laundry.

Most of the time when he called for me at night it was because he needed to urinate or move his bowels. By the time I was able to respond, he had often already wet the bed or shat himself. He would scold and scold me, accusing me of purposely waiting to enter so he would soil himself. In my exhausted state, I had to change all the bedding and undress him and wash up the bed and clean his body and then put him into fresh clothes. The smell was often so foul it made me gag. This process was exhausting, intimate, and awful.

Yet it was the strangest thing. When I was washing up his shit and piss, stripping down the bed of its soiled sheets, Songnian was happy. More than that. He was pos-itively gleeful! He was not humiliated. Not in the least! It was *me* who felt a stifling intimacy and convulsive dis-gust. I didn't grasp it at the time—it was as though he was beyond such considerations. Or perhaps it was that our dynamic did not admit them; I was his disciple. It was my duty to take care of him. To follow him absolutely.

To serve. I was the one who had embarrassed myself. I had failed him. I hadn't come in time. His incontinence made *me* feel ashamed. And he knew it.

"You think that I'm trying to humiliate you by making you clean up my shit," he said with an inexplicable smirk.

"No, Shifu. It's not that. I'm so sorry that I came in late." I bowed and bowed, eyes downcast. I was twenty-two years old. What was I supposed to make of all this? I never imagined that *this* was what my monastic training would involve.

I was completely exhausted, beaten down by his lectures and scolding. Burned to the ground. I sometimes felt like giving up. I took a deep breath and told myself to relax. To come back to the present moment. To do my work. To help. To respond in whatever circumstances that I found myself.

Later, when my photo was all over the papers, and my court case was dragging on, I realized the old monk was still teaching me. He had been preparing me for what I would endure. This face is nothing. Humiliation is nothing. What a lesson in staying in the present moment. Of maintaining equanimity. In keeping my bodhisattva vows and responding compassionately. Songnian was planting the capacity to make peace with whatever life threw at me, although I didn't know it at the time.

25

Waking Up the World

ONE NIGHT, after the seminar with Ajahn Brahm, I drove back quite late. By the time I reached Chan Forest it was nearly midnight. I was sitting in the front seat of the car, next to the driver, as we sped through the night. The vast cityscape of Jakarta's brightly lit buildings went on and on. And then finally we passed into the countryside, and I could see the moon and stars and the soft light coming from small houses and huts.

For some reason I was touched. I thought of my *shifu*, Master Sheng Yen, and one of the last times I had driven with him before he passed on. He was teaching at the Dharma Drum Retreat Center in Pine Bush, a drive of over two hours from the main Chan meditation center in Queens where we were staying.

We left very early in the morning. Sheng Yen sat in front next to the driver. I was his attendant and sat in back. At that point, he was already quite ill.

He taught during the day and there were also meetings. We had to return to Queens that night. It was already dusk when we set out after dinner. Heavy traffic on the roads meant it was quite late by the time we came back into the city. The bright lights were all around. The dark outline of Shifu's head and neck were in front of me. The driver was looking straight ahead and everyone was quiet. Sitting behind Shifu that night—it is very difficult to describe my feelings. The car was quiet. The world flashed by. Everything was moving, but inside the car it was so still. Outside it was cold; inside the car was warm. The driver drove carefully, not making any sudden brakes or turns to disturb Sheng Yen. When I shifted in my seat, I did so slowly and carefully so as not to upset the cocoon-like feeling of the car's cabin. I tried to make my breath as light as possible, so soft that it was inaudible.

Looking at Sheng Yen's silhouette, the words of the four great vows rose inside me. We do these vows before each meal, before the morning and evening service, after waking up and before going to bed:

> Sentient beings are innumerable, I vow
>   to deliver them all.
> Vexations are endless, I vow to eliminate
>   them all.
> Approaches to the Dharma are limitless, I vow
>   to master them all.
> Buddhahood is supreme, I vow to attain it.

I had been reciting these vows seven times a day for many years, but they had never quite reverberated inside me the way they did that night on the journey back to Queens. I felt the full weight of Sheng Yen's deep determination and strength, the unbreakable power of his commitment. He was so determined to help. To wake up the world. He was in constant motion, a ranger of the Dharma, always traveling to spread the teachings. The vows to which he gave his life were paradoxes, unsolvable contradictions. Yet he had an unshakable certainty that the impossibilities they asked of us were possible. How could that be? We traveled on through the vast and glittering city. Innumerable. Inexhaustible. Endless. Impossible! And yet unshakable. An absolute commitment and belief in the path.

In these last years of his life I often wondered whether people actually understood what he was trying to teach them—a refrain that often went through my head as I watched him work day in and day out, exhausting himself. Was it worth it? I suppose that I wanted him to slow down and take better care of himself. But there was no stopping him.

"It's a race against time, and I'm almost at the finish line, the end of my life. No time to stop now. Whatever I can complete in this life, I will do it. What I can't accomplish, I will do in my next life," he told me.

Nonetheless, I had my doubts. After a particularly punishing trip, I voiced them: "We fly here, fly there. Is it worth it? Do people really understand?"

"Not our problem. Our job is to teach the Dharma," he replied.

I did not yet have the life experience to understand what it is to give and keep giving. To give, as he did, unconditionally, expecting nothing in return.

Our vows are inconceivable, unattainable, beyond conception. Yet now I know, as Sheng Yen did, that they are possible. He gave his life to them. He held nothing, absolutely nothing, back. He gave without reservation. With total commitment. Endlessly, innumerably, inexhaustibly—with his body, speech, and mind. And with the goodness, the limitless goodness, of his heart.

About the Authors

AJAHN BRAHM (Ajahn Brahma-vamso Mahathera), born Peter Betts in London in 1951, is a Theravada Buddhist monk. Ajahn Brahm grew up in London and earned a degree in theoretical physics from Cambridge University. Disillusioned with the world of academe, he trained as a monk in the jungles of Thailand under Ajahn Chah. A monk for over thirty years, Ajahn Brahm is a revered spiritual guide and the abbot of Bodhinyana Monastery, in Serpentine, Western Australia—one of the largest monasteries in the southern hemisphere. He is also the spiritual director of the Buddhist Society of Western Australia, and spiritual adviser and inspiration for Buddhist centers throughout Asia and Australia. His winning combination of wit and wisdom makes his books bestsellers in many languages, and on his teaching tours Brahm regularly draws multinational audiences of thousands. He's the author of *The Art of Disappearing: The Buddha's Path to Lasting Joy*; *Mindfulness, Bliss, and*

Beyond: A Meditator's Handbook; Who Ordered This Truck-load of Dung: Inspiring Stories for Welcoming Life's Difficulties; Don't Worry, Be Grumpy: Inspiring Stories for Making the Most of Each Moment; Kindfulness; and *Bear Awareness: Questions and Answers on Taming Your Wild Mind.*

MASTER GUOJUN was born in Singapore in 1974 and ordained as a monk under Ven. Songnian of Mahabodhi Temple, Singapore. He is one of the youngest Dharma heirs of the renowned Chan master Sheng Yen. He has practiced meditation intensively since 1997. He has studied Tibetan Buddhism and Theravada Buddhism, as well as various aspects of the Mahayana tradition. Master Guojun is also a spiritual and guiding teacher of Chan Community Canada and Chan Indonesia. He was the abbot of Dharma Drum Retreat Center in Pine Bush, New York, from 2005 to 2008. He is the author of *Essential Chan Buddhism*, which has been published in several languages, and *Chan Heart, Chan Mind*. He is currently the president of Mahabodhi Monastery in Singapore.

What to Read Next
from Wisdom Publications

CHAN HEART, CHAN MIND
A Meditation on Serenity and Growth
Master Guojun with Kenneth Wapner

"Simple, lovely writing, vivid detail, and understanding of the Chan path give this short book a gentle spirit."
—*Publishers Weekly*

DON'T WORRY, BE GRUMPY
Inspiring Stories for Making the Most of Each Moment
Ajahn Brahm

"If a picture is worth a thousand words, then a good metaphorical story is worth that many more. Ajahn Brahm's latest collection of stories is funny, endearing, and, of course, infused with wisdom."—Arnie Kozak, author of *Wild Chickens and Petty Tyrants*

WHO ORDERED THIS TRUCKLOAD OF DUNG?
Inspiring Stories for Welcoming Life's Difficulties
Ajahn Brahm

"Ajahn Brahm is the Seinfeld of Buddhism."—Sumi Loundon Kim, author of *Sitting Together*

KINDFULNESS
Ajahn Brahm

"Readers will find the book's simple, gentle language and short chapters—with the most important points boldfaced—easy to follow. Perhaps following this gentle guide to countercultural thinking will bring some needed peace to a harried world."—*Publishers Weekly*

BEAR AWARENESS
Questions and Answers on Taming Your Wild Mind
Ajahn Brahm

"I wish all my favorite teachers would offer a book in question and answer format. It creates an intimate setting, as if the reader is in the room with Ajahn Brahm. In addition, almost all the questions are ones that practitioners have at one time or another. Have you ever wondered how ego affects your meditation or whether meditation can replace sleep at night? Read this book and get the answers from one of today's foremost Buddhist teachers."—Toni Bernhard, author of *How to Be Sick*

MINDFULNESS, BLISS, AND BEYOND
A Meditator's Handbook
Ajahn Brahm
Foreword by Jack Kornfield

"Riveting and real. I can't tell you how thrilled I was to read it."—Glenn Wallis, translator of *The Dhammapada*

THE ART OF DISAPPEARING
The Buddha's Path to Lasting Joy
Ajahn Brahm

"This book is an invaluable companion for your journey to your true self, the not-self that lies at the end of the Buddha's path."—BuddhaSpace

TOUCHING GROUND
Devotion and Demons along the Path to Enlightenment
Tim Testu
Edited by Emma Varvaloucas
Introduction by Jeanette Testu
Foreword by Jaimal Yogis

"A wonderful addition to a cherished genre: the spiritual memoir of the all-too-human, struggling practitioner, heroically seeking a way to transcend their flaws and challenges, to achieve a moment of blessed liberation. I suspect you'll enjoy it as much as I did. —Josh Korda, guiding teacher of Dharma Punx NYC and author of *Unsubscribe*

About Wisdom Publications

Wisdom Publications is the leading publisher of classic and contemporary Buddhist books and practical works on mindfulness. To learn more about us or to explore our other books, please visit our website at wisdomexperience.org or contact us at the address below.

Wisdom Publications
199 Elm Street
Somerville, MA 02144 USA

We are a 501(c)(3) organization, and donations in support of our mission are tax deductible.

Wisdom Publications is affiliated with the Foundation for the Preservation of the Mahayana Tradition (FPMT).